W9-BHI-987

THE FUTURE
OF
ISRAEL

JIMMY SWAGGART

THE FUTURE

OF

ISRAEL

JIMMY SWAGGART

JIMMY SWAGGART MINISTRIES
P.O. Box 262550 | Baton Rouge, Louisiana 70826-2550
www.jsm.org

ISBN 978-1-941403-67-9

09-138 | COPYRIGHT © 2019 Jimmy Swaggart Ministries®

19 20 21 22 23 24 25 26 27 28/ Sheridan / 10 9 8 7 6 5 4 3 2 1

All rights reserved. Printed and bound in U.S.A.

No part of this publication may be reproduced in any form or
by any means without the publisher's prior written permission.

TABLE OF CONTENTS

INTRODUCTION

INTRODUCTION

ISRAEL APPEARS AS A thorn in the side of the world. In other words, most of the world just wishes that Israel would go away. To be frank, most of the world wouldn't care very much (if at all) if the Muslims totally destroyed Israel. Why this animosity? Why this ill will? Why this attitude?

Israel is a long way from God, meaning that she is in a perilous situation respecting her spiritual condition. Despite that fact, God still has a plan for Israel, which is aptly outlined in His Word. In other words, Israel is ultimately and eventually going to carry out what God planned for her so many thousands of years ago. In effect, Israel will ultimately be the leading nation in the world. This will be in the time of the kingdom age and the time when Israel will have fully and totally accepted the Lord Jesus Christ not only as Messiah, but as Saviour and Lord.

A SIGN

When Israel was destroyed as a nation in AD 70, and then was totally and completely destroyed in AD 135, the people were then scattered all over the world. Then nearly 2,000 years later, they were brought back to form a nation in the same geographical area as in Bible times. Nothing like that has ever been done in history. No other people has ever been scattered all over the world and then, nearly 2,000 years later, come together to form a union and a nation, and that was after a holocaust of unprecedented proportions. It had never happened before in history, and that alone should give the world the knowledge that God is behind these people. It could not have been done without the leading and guidance of the Holy Spirit, and that was despite the fact that Israel has rejected the Lord Jesus.

About 3,500 years ago, a backslidden prophet by the name of Balaam stated of Israel, *"For from the top of the rocks I see him, and from the hills I behold him: lo, the people shall dwell alone, and shall not be reckoned among the nations"* (Num. 23:9).

So it has been from then until now. Israel is different than any nation in the world, and it is because they are the chosen of God. Admittedly and as stated, they have been away from the Lord for a long, long time; however, that is soon to change, which will take place at the second coming.

THE THEOLOGY OF ISRAEL

There are some so-called Christians who have written Israel off. They claim that this little spit of land in the Middle East called Israel, has no spiritual significance whatsoever. They claim that Israel, in the crucifixion of Christ, sealed her doom, and the church has now taken her place.

In a sense, it is true that the church has taken her place, but that does not mean that what God originally intended for Israel will not yet come to pass. It most definitely will! How anyone could read the Bible and see the multitude of promises made by God regarding the restoration of Israel, and then deny what the Bible plainly states, is a mystery to me. Israel will be restored, and no, as far as supremacy is concerned, the church has not taken her place.

Paul plainly told us that in the mind of God, Israel is the superior in her place and position as it regards the church.

Listen to Paul: *"I say then, Has God cast away His people? God forbid. For I also am an Israelite, of the seed of Abraham, of the tribe of Benjamin. God has not cast away His people which He foreknew"* (Rom. 11:1-2). Then Paul said:

And if some of the branches be broken off (not all of the branches, but some; referring to the fact that Israel will ultimately be brought back), *and you* (refers to the church, i.e., 'the Gentiles'), *being a wild olive tree* (inferior), *were grafted in among them* (presents the inferior—the church—being grafted into the superior—Israel—which is totally against nature), *and with them partake of the root and fatness of the olive tree* (means that the church derives its life from the common root that was originally given to Israel of long ago); *Boast not against the branches* (the church has not replaced Israel in the plan of God, even though the church is included in the plan of God due to Israel's rejection of Christ). *But if you boast, you bear not the root, but the root you* (as stated, the church was grafted in and is built upon the promises originally given to Israel, which still apply to Israel and one day will be fulfilled). *You will say then, The branches were broken off, that I might be grafted in* (the church must ever know and understand that it was and is second choice). *Well; because of unbelief they* (Israel) *were broken off* (unbelief respecting Christ and the cross), *and you stand by faith* (proclaims that the church was brought in because of faith and not merit, and stands in its present position by faith and not merit). *Be not high-minded, but fear* (the reason is given in the next verse)*: For if God spared not the natural branches* (Israel), *take heed lest He also spare not you* (again refers to the church, as is obvious) (Rom. 11:17-21) (The Expositor's Study Bible).

ANOTHER WAY OF SALVATION?

Then on the other side of the spectrum, there are some preachers who claim that even though Israel has rejected Jesus Christ, God has provided another way of salvation for them, meaning the law. No, He hasn't! There is only one way of salvation, whether it's for Jew or it's for Gentile, and that is the acceptance of Jesus Christ as Saviour and Lord. Jesus plainly said, and rightly so, *"I am the way, the truth, and the life: no man comes unto the Father, but by Me"* (Jn. 14:6).

Jesus made it crystal clear.

Preachers who insinuate that God has another plan of salvation for the Jews other than Christ are not doing the Jewish people a favor. Not at all! With love and kindness, Jews, as well as Gentiles, should be pointed to Christ. Due to the fact of what Jesus did at the cross, there is no other way of salvation. That must be settled in our hearts and minds without question.

HARD DAYS AHEAD

Due to her rejection of Jesus Christ, Israel has seen some terrible days in the past, with the Holocaust certainly not being the least of this terrible time; however, the time just ahead, called the great tribulation, will be worse even than the Holocaust. In fact, it will be the worst time that Israel has ever seen in her checkered history.

Jesus said: *"For then shall be great tribulation, such as was not since the beginning of the world to this time, no, nor ever shall be. And except those days should be shortened, there should no flesh be saved: but for the elect's* (Israel's) *sake those days shall be shortened* (by the second coming)" (Mat. 24:21-22).

It is hard to imagine that something could be worse than the Holocaust, but Jesus said it would be. During the time of the great tribulation, the Antichrist will attempt to do what Haman, Herod, and Hitler failed to do. He will come close to succeeding. The great prophet Zechariah said that in this coming time, two-thirds of the population of Israel will be slaughtered (Zech. 13:8).

THE REPENTANCE OF ISRAEL

This repentance will take place immediately after the second coming of the Lord. At the beginning they will know that this is their true Messiah, but at the first will not recognize Him as the one they crucified—the Lord Jesus Christ. After a short period of time, they will know.

The Lord says the following: *"And I will pour upon the house of David and upon the inhabitants of Jerusalem, the Spirit of grace and of supplications: and they shall look upon Me whom they have pierced, and they shall mourn for Him, as one mourns for his only son, and shall be in bitterness for Him, as one that is in bitterness for his firstborn"* (Zech. 12:10).

"And I will pour" refers to the Lord pouring out fire upon Zion's adversaries but the Holy Spirit upon her inhabitants (II Thess. 1). If one is to notice, the Messiah Himself is speaking in the entirety of this chapter as far as the word pierced; then the Holy Spirit points to the moral effect produced by the revelation. *"Upon the house of David,"* proclaims the promise originally given to David concerning his seed upon the throne of Israel (II Sam. 7:12-16).

THE SPIRIT OF GRACE

The phrase, *"And I will pour upon the house of David and upon the inhabitants of Jerusalem, the Spirit of grace,"* concerns the goodness of God and means they are no longer trusting in their law, but instead, the grace of God, which is found only in the Lord Jesus Christ. *"And I will pour upon the house of David and upon the inhabitants of Jerusalem, the Spirit of ... supplications,"* speaks of Israel supplicating the Lord and the Lord supplicating the Father on their behalf. The word means "to ask humbly and earnestly."

"And they shall look upon Me whom they have pierced," identifies who and what they are, and who He is. *"And they shall mourn for Him, as one mourns for his only son,"* now proclaims the moral effect produced by this revelation as given by the Holy Spirit. They will then make their supplications to Him for mercy and forgiveness.

"And shall be in bitterness for Him," means "a sense of intense shame." It speaks of true repentance.

The last phrase, *"As one that is in bitterness for his firstborn,"* refers to the loss of an only son, the firstborn. In effect, they killed their own son, and the firstborn at that, which meant that the family line could not continue. It was, in fact, destroyed, at least as far as the covenant was concerned; however, this Son, or firstborn, rose from the dead. Even though they would not accept it then, they will accept it now—and because He lives, they shall live also!

THE MANNER OF ISRAEL'S REPENTANCE

"In that day shall there be a great mourning in Jerusalem, as the mourning of Hadad-rimmon in the valley of Megiddon."

As Zechariah 12:10 proclaims, there is personal mourning, with national mourning in verse 11, and domestic mourning in verses 12 through 14. Every man will feel himself guilty of piercing Immanuel, which is the way they should feel.

The last phrase refers to King Josiah being killed in this place (II Chron. 35:22-25). His reign was the one gleam of light in the gloom that covered the nation from Manasseh to the captivity. Consequently, there was great mourning respecting his death.

"And the land shall mourn, every family apart; the family of the house of David apart, and their wives apart; the family of the house of Nathan apart, and their wives apart; The family of the house of Levi apart, and their wives apart; the family of Shimei apart, and their wives apart" (Zech. 12:12-13).

The house of David and Nathan speaks of the princely line of Israel, while the family of Levi and Shimei speaks of the priests. Consequently, these two verses proclaim a personal and general repentance on the part of both the civil and spiritual leadership.

"All the families that remain, every family apart, and their wives apart" (Zech. 12:14).

"All the families that remain," speaks now of the balance of Israel. Judah's repentance and conversion will not be motivated by fear of punishment, but by the overwhelming sense of guilt affecting the heart when they recognize that their deliverer is Jesus whom they crucified, and that all along, despite their hatred and their conduct, He kept on loving them!

THE FOUNTAIN OF CLEANSING FOR ISRAEL

"In that day there shall be a fountain opened to the house of David and to the inhabitants of Jerusalem for sin and for uncleanness" (Zech. 13:1).

"In that day," occurs 18 times in Zechariah 9-14. This shows how precious that day is to the Messiah's heart. In that day,

His victory over the enemies of His people will be great, but greater will be His moral victory over His people themselves.

The Christian's true triumphs are God's triumphs over him, and God's triumphs over His people are our only victories. Such was Jacob of old, who represented Israel in the coming glad day. The conversion of the apostle Paul also illustrates the future conversion of Israel. He hated Jesus, but on the Damascus Road, he looked upon Him whom he had pierced and, thereby, mourned and wept.

The phrase, *"In that day there shall be a fountain opened,"* does not mean that it is first opened there, but that Israel will only begin to partake of it in that day, i.e., the beginning of the kingdom age. This fountain was historically opened at Calvary, but it will be consciously opened to repentant Jews in the future day of her repentance, for the fact and function of that fountain only becomes conscious to the awakened sinner.

A true sense of sin and guilt in relationship to God awakens the sense of need of cleansing, and so the shed and cleansing blood of the Lamb of God becomes precious to the convicted conscience. As well, the ever-living efficacy of Christ's atoning work, with its power to cleanse the conscience and the life, is justly comparable to a fountain and not to a font. The sense of the Hebrew text is that this fountain shall be opened and shall remain open.

JERUSALEM SINNERS

"To the house of David and to the inhabitants of Jerusalem for sin and for uncleanness," portrays the possibility that, of all sinners,

the Jerusalem sinners may be accounted the greatest. It was Jerusalem that stoned the prophets and crucified the Messiah; therefore, great sinners may hope for great pardon and cleansing in this fountain opened for the house of David.

The entrance of Christ judges sin, unmasks its true character, and arouses a moral consciousness which approves that judgment. That entrance dominates, adjusts, disciplines, instructs, and cleanses man's affections, relationships, and desires. All of this must be cleansed, not only in Israel of a future day, but also in any and all who come to Christ. That fountain is open to all. (Most of the material on Israel's repentance was derived from George Williams.)

In this effort, we will attempt to show you how the Holy Spirit works as it regards the bringing of Israel to this place of repentance. Israel, as most, will not give up easily or quickly; however, ultimately, she will fall at the feet of the world's Redeemer. Actually, He will be the one she nailed to a cross nearly 2,000 years ago. Then Israel will fulfill her role as laid down in the Word of God.

Trust on! Trust on believer!
Though long the conflict be
Thou yet shalt prove victorious;
Thy God shall fight for thee.

Trust on! Trust on; Thy failings
May bow thee to the dust,
But in thy deepest sorrow,
O give not up thy trust.

Trust on! The danger presses;
Temptation strong is near,
Yet o'er life's dangerous rapids,
He shall thy passage steer.

O Christ is strong to save us,
He is a faithful Friend,
Trust on! Trust on! believer,
O trust Him to the end.

CHAPTER 1

PROPHECY

PROPHECY

"ALSO, YOU SON OF MAN, *prophesy unto the mountains of Israel, and say, You mountains of Israel, hear the word of the* LORD: *Thus says the Lord* GOD; *Because the enemy has said against you, Aha, even the ancient high places are ours in possession: Therefore prophesy and say, Thus says the Lord* GOD; *Because they have made you desolate, and swallowed you up on every side, that you might be a possession unto the residue of the heathen, and you are taken up in the lips of talkers, and are an infamy of the people: Therefore, you mountains of Israel, hear the word of the Lord* GOD; *Thus says the Lord* GOD *to the mountains, and to the hills, to the rivers, and to the valleys, to the desolate wastes, and to the cities that are forsaken, which became a prey and derision to the residue of the heathen who are round about; Therefore thus says the Lord* GOD; *Surely in the fire of My jealousy have I spoken against the residue of the heathen, and against all Idumea, which have appointed My land into their possession with the joy of all their heart, with despiteful minds, to cast it out for a prey"* (Ezek. 36:1-5).

PROPHECY

Williams says, "The double prophecy of this chapter predicts the restoration of the land of Israel and of the people of Israel; and the fundamental moral principle is taught that inward holiness must precede outward prosperity."[1]

There was a limited fulfillment of these prophecies at the restoration under Zerubbabel, but their total fulfillment (actually that to which these prophecies point) is yet future.

God chastens His people, but He destroys their enemies. His people's shame is temporary; that of their enemies, perpetual. The sense of Ezekiel 36:3 is that the heathen charged Jehovah with inability to protect His land.

PROPHESY UNTO THE MOUNTAINS OF ISRAEL

The heading has to do with that which pertains to the land of Israel and what the Lord will ultimately do there.

Actually, this prophecy is divided into two parts: Ezekiel 36:1-5, which connects to the previous chapter about Israel's restoration as it deals with the land; and Ezekiel 36:6-14, which deals with the people.

The phrase of verse 2, *"Because the enemy has said against you, Aha,"* portrays this enemy as Edom. They gloated over the fall of Judah and Jerusalem, and did so to all who would hear. What they didn't realize was that their gloat against the people of Israel was a gloat against God—to slander that which belongs to God is to slander God! As well, as should be overly obvious, the Lord notes all that takes place, even down to the guttural slurs. He does not take kindly to such being leveled at His people, irrespective of their spiritual condition.

THE TALKERS

The phrase of Ezekiel 36:3, *"And you are taken up in the lips of talkers, and are an infamy of the people,"* constitutes the only place in the Bible where the word *talkers* is found. The Hebrew word is *lashon,* which means "a fork of flames; babbler; evil speaker; accuser; slanderer; to calumniate or wag the tongue," all of which speak of Satan's chief efforts to destroy God's people as *"the accuser of our brethren"* (Rev. 12:10).

I would certainly trust that from all of this, the reader understands the severity of the situation at hand. When one hears the gossip peddled by many Christians, it becomes quickly obvious that they have never read the book of Ezekiel.

When a person comes to Christ, he can do so only by virtue of who Christ is and what He has done for us at the cross. We *"are bought with a price"* (I Cor. 6:20; 7:23), in fact, a price of such magnitude as to defy all description—the death of the Son of God on the cross of Calvary, which alone could atone for all sin.

Having accepted Christ and now becoming His children, we are *"heirs of God, and joint-heirs with* (Jesus) *Christ"* (Rom. 8:17).

Belonging exclusively to the Lord, we are guaranteed His watchful care. As you do not appreciate at all someone leveling charges against your children, that is, if you have children, likewise, the Lord does not appreciate it when someone levels charges, or even curses, against one for whom He has paid such a price.

Some people think that because they are Christian, likewise, bought with a price, that gives them the right to level charges against another Christian. To say the least, it doesn't. In fact, I personally feel that the Lord looks with even greater disdain on the Christian who would do such a thing because he should know better.

THE MINISTRY OF RECONCILIATION

The phrase in Ezekiel 36:4, *"Thus says the Lord GOD to the mountains, and to the hills, to the rivers, and to the valleys, to the desolate wastes, and to the cities that are forsaken,"* proclaims the fact that what the Lord has chastised, He can restore. Again, God chastens His people, but He destroys their enemies. God chastens His people, but He destroys their enemies. Anything the Lord does with His people, whatever direction it might take, is that they may be ultimately brought to a place of victory. If repentance is needed, He works toward that end. Sometimes He must chastise the individual, and, in fact, He chastises all believers, and for the obvious reasons (Heb. 12:5–11). If the Christian loses faith and begins to drift away, the Holy Spirit continues to make every effort to pull that believer back to the desired place.

Actually, one of the great ministries of the Holy Spirit and one of the most important is the ministry of reconciliation, which includes restoration. In fact, before restoration can be brought about, reconciliation must have already taken place.

THE ENMITY

Before the Lord can do such with Israel, or any individual for that matter, the enmity, or quarrel, must be bridged over. It implies that the parties being reconciled were formerly hostile to one another. The Bible tells us bluntly that sinners are *"enemies"* of God (Rom. 5:10; Col. 1:21; James 4:4).

We must not minimize the seriousness of these and similar passages. An enemy is not someone who comes a little short of being a friend. He is in the other camp. He is altogether opposed. The New Testament, as well as the Old, pictures God in vigorous opposition to everything and anything that is evil.

The only way to overcome enmity is to take away the cause of the quarrel. That cause is sin. Christ died to put away our sin. In this way He dealt with the enmity between man and God. He put it out of the way. He made the way wide open for men to come back to God. He did it all at the cross! It is this that is described by the term *reconciliation*, which brings about restoration.

MAN'S SIN

It is interesting to notice that no New Testament passage speaks of Christ as reconciling God to man. Always, the stress is on man being reconciled. In the nature of the case, this is very important. It is man's sin that has caused the enmity. It is man's sin that has to be dealt with. Actually, man feels no hostility toward God on account of his sin. The barrier arises because God demands holiness in man. Therefore, what Jesus did at Calvary was far more than defeating Satan and the powers of darkness, but His death, as well, assuaged the anger of God and satisfied the debt piled up by man and owed to God. Consequently, Calvary was brought about to satisfy the righteous demands of a thrice-holy God. In atoning for all sin, our Lord, likewise, totally and completely defeated Satan. While the cross was totally and completely Satan's undoing, that was in actuality only a by-product of what the cross accomplished.

The main purpose of the cross was to address man's sin—the terrible debt of sin owed by man to God. It was a debt, incidentally, that man could not pay. So, if the debt was to be paid and, thereby, the judgment lifted, God would have to become man and pay the debt Himself, which He did by going to the cross.

WHY NOT ANOTHER FORM OF SACRIFICE?

No, it had to be a cross, and there was a reason for that.

Under the law of Moses, if an Israelite committed a dastardly crime, He was to be stoned to death, and then his body was to be placed on a tree and hang there as a spectacle for all to see. This showed that he was cursed by God; however, he was not to hang there all night, only for a few hours, and then was to be taken down (Deut. 21:22–23).

The death of Christ was not an execution, and neither was it an assassination. The death of Christ was a sacrifice, with Christ purposefully and willingly laying down His life. If it was to be a sacrifice, this is the way it had to be (Jn. 10:17–18).

As well, this sacrifice must be for all sin, even the worst sin that one could ever begin to think (I Cor. 6:9–11), and, as well, the very cause of sin (Jn. 1:29).

This was so much planned and recognized by the Lord that the Holy Spirit through Peter said, as he spoke to Israel about Jesus, *"Whom you slew and hanged on a tree"* (Acts 5:30).

He also spoke through Paul, saying, *"And when they had fulfilled all that was written of Him, they took Him down from the tree, and laid Him in a sepulchre"* (Acts 13:29).

Peter also said, *"Who His own self bare our sins in His own body on the tree, that we, being dead to sins, should live unto righteousness: by whose stripes you were healed"* (I Pet. 2:24).

THE CROSS

As we've already stated, the Lord revealed to Abraham the way that redemption would be afforded, which would be by death (Gen. 22); however, it was to Moses that He revealed what manner this death would be, which would be the cross (Num. 21).

If it is to be remembered, Jesus was placed on the cross at 9 a.m., which was the time of the morning sacrifice, and He died at 3 p.m., the time of the evening sacrifice. As well, His body was taken down from the cross before nightfall, totally fulfilling the Scripture regarding Deuteronomy 21:22–23.

While the malefactor was cursed by God, even as Moses said, Jesus, instead, bearing our sin on the cross, was *"made a curse for us,"* which is totally different (Gal. 3:13). To be cursed of God, one would have had to have committed the sin, whatever it may have been. Christ committed no sin, so He had to be made a curse, which means that He suffered the penalty we should have suffered, which was death (Jn. 3:16).

Even though Christ most definitely suffered on the cross, it was not so much the suffering that redeemed humanity. Even though He was greatly humiliated on the cross, likewise, it was not humiliation that redeemed us.

REDEMPTION

It was the giving of Himself as a sacrifice and the fact that He was perfect in every respect, which provided a sacrifice that God could accept as payment. It was payment—the life of Christ poured out regarding His shed blood (Eph. 2:13–18) —that atoned for all sin—past, present, and future. There are three Greek words, at least the three most often used, which typify redemption:

1. *Garazo.* This refers to the price being paid and, thereby, the slave being purchased out of the marketplace.
2. *Exgarazo.* This refers to the fact that the price was so adequately paid that the person purchased out of the slave market of sin, thereby, a captive of Satan, will never again have to be worried about being placed on that particular auction block, so to speak.
3. *Lutroo.* Indicates that such a price was paid that in eternity future, angels, whether fallen or otherwise, will never be able to say that the price was insufficient.

As well, this new covenant, which totally and completely fulfilled the old covenant, thereby, retiring that great legislation, is so perfect, so complete, and so total that the Holy Spirit through Paul referred to it as *"the everlasting covenant,"* meaning that in eternity future, it will never have to be amended (Heb. 13:20).

LOVE

In all of this, we must make it clear that the anger of God against man because of his sin never changes His love for man. The Bible is very clear that God's love to man never varies, no matter what man may do; indeed, the whole atoning work of Christ stems from God's great love.

It was *"while we were yet sinners"* that *"Christ died for us"* (Rom. 5:8).

The truth must be zealously guarded. At the same time, we must not allow ourselves to slip into the position of maintaining that God overlooks sin. That He cannot do! Between God and man there must be reconciliation. Reconciliation is a purely personal matter concerning man's need. Reconciliation in some sense was effected outside man before anything happened within man. This speaks of the finished work of Calvary. A reconciliation that can be received must be offered and, thus, in some sense already accomplished.

Israel will experience reconciliation and restoration immediately after the second coming of Christ. The prophet Zechariah records this event (Zech. 12:10–14; 13:1–2). Then the enmity will be removed, which will then pave the way for a total restoration to be carried out.

JEALOUSY!

The phrase of Ezekiel 36:5, *"Surely in the fire of My jealousy have I spoken against the residue of the heathen,"* refers to anger at a white-hot pitch.

Edom not only proposed to take *"My land,"* but to do so with a gleeful joy and with despiteful minds, i.e., with contempt of soul, meaning that Edom held Judah in contempt and, as well, Judah's God, Jehovah.

God is jealous over His people and, in fact, all that He is or has. This means that believers belong to Him, and that He doesn't take kindly to someone else attempting to hurt His property or even take His property. Such, as should be obvious, is a dead-end street. In other words, all who enter that street don't come back!

"Prophesy therefore concerning the land of Israel, and say unto the mountains, and to the hills, to the rivers, and to the valleys, Thus says the Lord GOD; Behold, I have spoken in My jealousy and in My fury, because you have borne the shame of the heathen" (Ezek. 36:6).

SHAME

The key to Ezekiel 36:6 is, *"You have borne the shame of the heathen."* This means, as it regards God's people, shame is temporary, while that of their enemies is perpetual.

The law of retribution is demanded by the absolute righteousness of God. The judicial visitations of God cannot possibly be one-sided. That which has been meted out to Israel for their sin would be meted out to Edom, as well as to all other opposing nations. The Palestinians should take note of this.

THE LIFTED HAND

The phrase of Ezekiel 36:7, *"I have lifted up My hand,"* refers to God taking an oath that what He had stated about the heathen and their punishment would most surely come to pass.

As well as ancient Edom, a present example is noted. I speak of the former Soviet Union.

This bastion of communism caused Christians who were in the Soviet Union to suffer terrible shame, as well as great persecution, throughout the entirety of its some 72-year reign.

Then, in 1989, and before the entire world, the Soviet Union disintegrated, producing a national shame, especially for communism, that was felt all around the world.

Sometimes the shame is slow in coming and sometimes rapidly so, as the example just given, but come it shall. The Lord has made a solemn vow, *"They shall bear their shame,"* and bear their shame they shall.

MORAL ELEVATION

The phrase of Ezekiel 36:8, *"O mountains of Israel,"* and *"the everlasting hills"* of Genesis 49:26 are terms expressive of the moral elevation of Israel over the physical elevation of Edom. In fact, Edom was mountainous. So this tells us that when Israel comes back to God, their moral elevation will be the highest of any nation in the world. They will come back to God at the second coming and will do so by accepting God's Son, the Lord Jesus Christ.

The phrase, *"For they are at hand to come,"* has the same connotation as *"lifted up My hand"* in Ezekiel 36:7. The Lord takes an oath that as He swore to punish Edom and even to make her desolate, conversely, He will bless Israel. This will be during the coming kingdom age.

PROSPERITY

The phrase of Ezekiel 36:9, *"tilled and sown,"* speaks of prosperity.

As the Lord said that He was against Edom (Ezek. 35:3), He, conversely, says of Israel, *"I am for you."*

Prosperity given by the Lord affects every part and parcel of one's life and living. First of all, there must be spiritual prosperity. This can be gained only by the believer properly placing his faith in the correct object, which must ever be the cross of Christ. Let's say it again:

- The only way to God is through Jesus Christ (Jn. 14:20).
- The only way to Christ is through the cross (Jn. 3:16; Eph. 2:13–18).
- The only way to the cross is through a denial of self (Lk. 9:23–24).

When spiritual prosperity becomes obvious, physical, financial, material, domestic, and social prosperity will then follow. The problem of the church, and especially in the last several decades, is that it has made financial prosperity its theme while ignoring the spiritual. Such is not to be, as such cannot be.

MULTIPLY

The phrase of Ezekiel 36:10, *"And I will multiply,"* proclaims the degree of blessing that will be given to Israel in that coming glad day.

As the Lord outlined the destruction of Edom and other nations, here He outlines the coming blessing and prosperity of the house of Israel. Then He said, *"even all of it,"* meaning that the entirety of the land would be blessed, which will incorporate both the northern and southern kingdoms, plus all of that which was originally promised to Abraham. It will take in Lebanon, Syria, about half of Iraq, the Sinai, and the Arabian Peninsula. This will be during the coming kingdom age.

BETTER

The phrase of Ezekiel 36:11, *"and will do better unto you than at your beginnings,"* proclaims the fact that as fruitful as Israel was, at least at times, in the remote past, it will be much more fruitful in the future. It will be a condition of prosperity so great that it should surpass any measure or degree of blessing previously enjoyed, not only by Israel, but any nation and every nation in the world that follows the Lord.

When one considers the blessing of the Lord on Israel under Solomon, which made it the premier nation in the world of that day, with silver being as rocks on the ground, then the magnitude of the coming blessing is on a scale little comprehended.

POSSESSION

Edom said they would possess the land, and the Lord says in Ezekiel 36:12 that *"My people Israel ... shall possess you,"* speaking of the land.

The phrase of verse 12, *"And you shall no more henceforth bereave them of men,"* means that all war will cease, which previously, and greatly so, thinned the ranks. Not only will there be no more war, but due to the trees that will grow beside the river that will proceed from under the threshold of the temple, death will be abolished (Ezek. 47:12).

THE LIE OF DARKNESS

The heathen had said, as Ezekiel 36:13 proclaims, *"Because they say unto you, Your land devours up men, and has bereaved your nations."* This proclaims the fact that the heathen spread the evil report that Israel devoured its inhabitants and was, therefore, cursed.

BLESSING

The phrase of Ezekiel 36:14, *"Therefore you shall devour men no more,"* pertains to the blessings that will come upon Israel during the coming kingdom age.

The idea of verse 14 is this: The great spiritual conflict between light and darkness had brought about the terrible contest for the land of Israel, which began immediately upon its inception and continued throughout its history. Even though the contest raged fiercely, with tremendous loss of life and destruction of property, still, it is doubtful if the nations fully understood, or even understood at all, the cause of the conflict.

In fact, that conflict rages even at this very moment, making Israel possibly the most dangerous place on earth. It is dangerous not only for what is taking place in the confines of its borders, but what it could bring about as it involves confrontation between other nations. So, the conflict remains and will remain, making the land of Israel the most dangerous place on earth, which will remain that way until the coming of the Lord. In fact, the danger is going to increase tremendously so in the near future, especially with the rise of the Antichrist.

THE WORD OF THE LORD

Ezekiel 36:15-16 proclaim the fact that Israel will be completely restored in the coming kingdom age, and that is beyond the shadow of a doubt. The Word of the Lord proclaims this fact, and to be sure, that which the Lord has spoken will definitely come true.

That God has ever stooped to use mere mortals to proclaim His glorious Word will ever be a mystery. It is the *"treasure in earthen vessels"* (II Cor. 4:7). The Word of the Lord is the only truth in the world and, in fact, ever has been.

THEIR OWN WAY

"Son of man, when the house of Israel dwelt in their own land, they defiled it by their own way and by their doings: their way was before me as the uncleanness of a removed woman" (Ezek. 36:17).

DEFILEMENT

- Verse 17 admits, *"their own way."* Man's way is defiling and defiles.
- The uncleanness of verse 17 pictures the vileness of the sinner in God's sight. The first statement of verse 29 declares the ability of the Saviour to fully cleanse the sinner.
- The argument of verses 19 and 20 is that not only did Israel profane Jehovah's name in the land prior to the exile, but they also profaned it among the heathen during the exile. Their conduct was so bad as captives that the heathen pointed at them with contempt and revulsion saying, *"These are the people of the LORD (Jehovah),"* etc. They profaned God by degrading Him

to companionship with the idols of the heathen and also by their immoral conduct.

The phrase of Ezekiel 36:17, *"They defiled it by their own way,"* refers to anything and everything that man does (even Christian man) that is done in his own strength and ability. This means that it's not strictly according to the Word of God, and it always defiles. As we have stated, man's way is defiling and defiles.

The phrase, *"their way was before Me as the uncleanness of a removed woman,"* pictures the vileness of the sinner in God's sight. The Lord is here using the symbolism of a woman's monthly period, which women undergo until the change of life. Spiritually, this is meant to symbolize the uncleanness of the heart due to the fall. It was used as an example of Israel's uncleanness.

Going back to man's ways, it must be readily understood that if the object of our faith is anything other than the cross, the Lord marks it down as spiritual uncleanness, which, of course, can never be accepted by the Lord. It is the cross, and the cross alone, that makes it possible for the righteousness of God to be freely imputed to the individual, whoever that individual may be. The righteousness of God, which is a pure, spotless, and unsullied righteousness, the only kind that God will accept, cannot be earned, cannot be merited, and cannot be purchased. It can only be received as a free gift and is predicated solely upon faith. By that we are speaking of faith in Christ and what Christ has done for us at the cross.

That is about as simple as simple can be; however, it is very difficult for man to accept, even religious man, and *especially* religious man.

THREE KINDS OF RIGHTEOUSNESS

There are three kinds of righteousness, to which the Word of God points, with only one being acceptable to the Lord. This is aptly described by Christ in the parable of the Pharisee and the publican. Jesus said:

> *Two men went up into the temple to pray; the one a Pharisee, and the other a publican. The Pharisee stood and prayed thus with himself, God, I thank You, that I am not as other men are, extortioners, unjust, adulterers, or even as this publican. I fast twice in the week, I give tithes of all that I possess. And the publican, standing afar off, would not lift up so much as his eyes unto heaven, but smote upon his breast, saying, God be merciful to me a sinner. I tell you, this man went down to his house justified rather than the other: for every one who exalts himself shall be abased; and he who humbles himself shall be exalted* (Lk. 18:10–14).

To be frank, the Pharisee of Jesus' day was accepted in Israel as being an excellent example of righteousness. By contrast, the publican, who was actually a tax collector, was looked at as the lowest of the low, with many in Israel thinking that those who functioned in such an occupation could not be saved. In effect, in one way or the other, these particular individuals were in the employ of Rome, which was abhorrent to Israel. So here we have the two men placed in total contrast, and done so by Christ in order to teach a most valuable lesson.

RELATIVE RIGHTEOUSNESS

Jesus drew attention first of all to relative righteousness. What is that?

The Pharisee compared himself to others as Luke 18:11 brings out, claiming that he was better than they were and, in fact, even better than the publican who stood some distance behind him, to whom we will address ourselves momentarily.

A great many in the modern church gauge their salvation or their walk with God relative to others. In other words, they pick out somebody who has done something very wrong, and because they have not done that thing, they automatically judge themselves as being more righteous than that person, whomever that person might be. Anytime we compare our righteousness to the righteousness of other people, whomever those people might be, we are, in fact, functioning from the position of relative righteousness, a righteousness, incidentally, that is self-righteousness, which God can never accept.

The church has a great problem in understanding how a Christian can do something wrong, and as bad as it might be, earnestly seek the Lord for mercy, grace, and forgiveness and, thereby, be declared perfectly righteous, and do so in a few moments' time. Few can accept that, which means they are rejecting the righteousness of God in favor of a man-devised righteousness. In no way is this meant to portray sin in a light manner. Sin is awful in any context and will always have an extremely negative effect upon the child of God if committed. That certainly should be understood and, in fact, well understood.

The truth is, there is no way the sinner can be saved or the Christian can be made right outside of the imputed righteousness of God, which is instantly given upon faith. Otherwise, he is placed in the ranks of the Pharisee with his relative righteousness.

WORKS RIGHTEOUSNESS

If one is practicing relative righteousness, it is certain that he will also be plagued with works righteousness.

What is that?

In Luke 18:12, the Pharisee said, *"I fast twice in the week, I give tithes of all that I possess,"* which means that his faith was resting in his works, which again, God cannot accept. He felt that his doing these things made him righteous in God's sight, which is the blight of the modern church and, in fact, has always been.

Regrettably, the far greater majority of the modern church is depending on a relative righteousness and a works righteousness. Momentarily, I will tell you how I know that.

Our Lord is not here demeaning the paying of tithes or fasting. Rather, He is condemning faith being placed in those things, and the thinking that doing of such earns us something with God.

In fact, every good Christian will pay his tithes and give offerings to the Lord. Every good Christian will, at times, fast. The idea is that our faith is not to be placed in those things, as helpful as they are in their own right.

IMPUTED RIGHTEOUSNESS

The publican could not boast of any of the things to which the Pharisee alluded. Even if he had done some good things, he never mentioned them, but only exclaimed to the Lord his true self as a sinner. Jesus said of this man that he *"would not lift up so much as his eyes unto heaven, but smote upon his breast, saying, God be merciful to me a sinner"* (Lk. 18:13).

Now, as the Lord was not condemning the paying of tithes and fasting, neither was He claiming that there is virtue in being a sinner. Quite the contrary! Our Lord was merely stating that the man admitted what he was, which, of course, God already knew, but which the Pharisee would not admit. The publican cried for mercy, and that's exactly what he received.

In fact, Jesus said that *"this man went down to his house justified rather than the other,"* with the *"other"* speaking of the Pharisee.

This means that the Lord instantly imputed a perfect righteousness to this man because he admitted what he was and because he asked for mercy. So, one moment the man was a sinner, which means that he had no righteousness at all, and the next moment he was totally righteous, having been imputed righteousness freely by the Lord, which is the only way that true righteousness can be granted and received.

RIGHTEOUSNESS AND THE CROSS

Now, the church, regrettably, has a difficult time accepting this. Let's look at it a little further. The believer must understand that everything we receive from the Lord, and I mean everything, is all made possible by Christ. He is always the source, and the cross is always the means.

This means that every single thing that Christ gives us, whatever it might be, comes to us exclusively through His sacrifice of Himself on the cross. In other words, the cross has made and makes it all possible. Before the cross, and I speak of Old Testament times, everything was granted to seeking souls on the basis of a work that was yet to be developed, i.e., the cross, all symbolized in the sacrifices. Since the cross, everything is given to us predicated on that finished work. Whatever we need, irrespective of what it might be, Christ has always had that commodity, be it righteousness or whatever; however, it is the cross that makes it possible for these things to be given to us. It is made possible simply because Jesus there atoned for all sin— past, present, and future—at least for all who will believe (Jn. 3:16).

THE HOLY SPIRIT

In fact, it is the Holy Spirit who perfects these things in our lives, and who alone can perfect these things. What He does is to take that which Christ has made possible by the cross and then bring it about in our lives according to our faith being placed in the correct object, which is the cross (Rom. 6:3-14; 8:1-11; Gal. 5; 6:14; I Cor. 1:17-18, 23; 2:2; Col. 2:14-15).

The Holy Spirit works exclusively within the confines of the parameters of the sacrifice of Christ, meaning that what Christ did at the cross gives the Holy Spirit the legal right to do the things that He does. Before the cross, He could only abide *"with"* the saints, but since the cross, He now abides *"in"* the saints, and does so permanently (Jn. 14:16-17).

THE FURY OF THE LORD

"Wherefore I poured My fury upon them for the blood that they had shed upon the land, and for their idols wherewith they had polluted it" (Ezek. 36:18).

This verse proclaims that the idol worship of Israel produced the shedding of blood in the offering of little children in human sacrifices. Because of this, the anger of the Lord knew no bounds. As a result and because they would not repent, He poured out His fury upon them. The fury of man is one thing, while the fury of God is something else altogether.

While all sin is awful in the eyes of God and should be awful in our eyes, as well, still, some sins are worse than others, as should be obvious. In other words, while God abhors all sin, there are certain sins that anger Him greatly. I think it should be understood that the offering of little children as human sacrifices would be one of the most egregious sins of all.

How could Israel do such a thing, especially considering that they gave the world the Word of God and, in fact, were the only people on the face of the earth who were privileged to have the Word of God?

All sin, and I speak of believers, always begins by the believer's faith being improperly placed. This was so before the cross, and it is certainly so after the cross (I Cor. 1:18, 23).

During this time, even while Israel was offering little children as human sacrifices, at the same time, they were offering up the lambs as sacrifices at the temple.

THE HARDENED HEART

The truth is that they had lost all understanding of what the sacrificial ritual actually meant. In fact, the ritual of offering animal sacrifices couldn't save anyone. It was that to which these sacrifices pointed, and which they symbolized, namely Christ and what He would do at the cross, that effected salvation. In fact, this meant that the object of faith for these Jews was meant to be the cross exactly as it is presently.

When they lost that understanding and treated the animal sacrifices as no more than a ceremony or a ritual, which means they had abandoned the cross, they were then an open target for Satan to take them ever deeper into sin, which he most definitely did.

It is the same presently. Whenever the object of faith is wrong for the child of God, whether before the cross or after the cross, the results will be the same—abject failure and unbelief!

One cannot trust Christ unless one has his faith anchored squarely in the cross. If the believer is not trusting Christ and the cross, failure will result, which is unavoidable. In fact, it will get worse and worse because an improper object of faith stops the Holy Spirit from performing His work within our lives. To be sure, without the full work of the Holy Spirit, the believer simply cannot live a successful Christian life.

SCATTERED

"And I scattered them among the heathen, and they were dispersed through the countries: according to their way and according to their doings I judged them" (Ezek. 36:19).

The phrase, *"And I scattered them among the heathen,"* not only concerned Ezekiel's day but, as well, concerned itself with AD 70 when Titus destroyed Jerusalem. This was done because they shed the blood of Christ. As a result, they were scattered all over the world and remained that way until 1948.

Actually, in a sense the majority of Jews are still scattered and will only be fully restored at the second coming of Christ.

THE PEOPLE OF THE LORD

"And when they entered unto the heathen, whither they went, they profaned My holy name, when they said to them, These are the people of the LORD, and are gone forth out of His land" (Ezek. 36:20).

The phrase, *"These are the people of the LORD,"* was actually said by the heathen and said in derision. In other words, it was said in scorn, bringing great reproach upon the Lord and, of course, upon His people, all which was purposefully intended.

Actually, the Jews were the only people of the Lord in the entirety of the world; however, their being defeated caused the heathen to conclude that Jehovah had either behaved capriciously toward His people and cast them off or had proven unequal to the task of protecting them. In either case, the honor of Jehovah had been lessened in the mind and tarnished by the words of the heathen. This, of course, had been brought about by Israel's sin.

THE HOLY NAME OF THE LORD

"But I had pity for My holy name, which the house of Israel had profaned among the heathen, whither they went" (Ezek. 36:21).

The phrase, *"But I had pity for My holy name,"* proclaims that the Lord will do certain positive things, not because of any good in Israel, but because of good in Himself.

Israel had become so corrupt, necessitating the destruction of themselves as a people and a nation, that there was no logical reason that they should be restored. They had not only profaned the name of the Lord in their own land but had also *"profaned* (it) *among the heathen, whither they went."*

However, for His holy name's sake and all it represented, which pertained to His promises and His Word, which He watches over even above all His name, Israel will be restored, as the following verses even unto the end of this chapter will proclaim. It will be for that reason and that reason alone that they will be restored.

Actually, the tenor of these statements constitutes the foundation of the great doctrine of grace. God saves man, not because He sees something good in man, but because there is something good in Himself. Even under the new covenant, which is predicated on grace, still, God's dealings with His family, the church, is predicated basically as it was with Israel of old. Much, if not all of what He does, is because of His own honor, which constitutes His name and His Word. The psalmist said, *"For You have magnified Your Word above all Your name"* (Ps. 138:2).

God's promises are wrapped up in His name, whereas His performance is wrapped up in His Word.

In other words, His performance is always greater than His promise.

Not saved are we by trying,
From self can come no aid:
'Tis on the blood relying,
Once for our ransom paid;
Tis looking unto Jesus,
The holy One and just;
'Tis His great work that saves us,
It is not Try, but Trust.

'Twas vain for Israel bitten,
By serpents on their way,
To look to their own doing,
That awful plague to stay;
The remedy for their healing,
When humbled in the dust,
Was of the Lord's revealing,
It was not Try, but Trust.

No deeds of ours are needed
To make Christ's merit more;
No frames of mind, or feelings,
Can add to His great store;
'Tis simply to receive Him,
The holy One and just,
'Tis as only to believe Him,
It is not Try, but Trust.

CHAPTER 2

A NEW HEART

A NEW HEART

"*THEREFORE SAY UNTO THE house of Israel, Thus says the Lord GOD; I do not this for your sakes, O house of Israel, but for My holy name's sake, which you have profaned among the heathen, whither you went*" (Ezek. 36:22).

THE NAME OF THE LORD

Four times in as many verses, the Holy Spirit through the prophet mentions the holy name of the Lord and how that Israel profaned it among the heathen, as Ezekiel 36:22 says.

In fact, if one is to notice, there is much repetition in what the Holy Spirit says through the prophet, even as it regards all of these prophecies. This is done by design.

Anything the Lord says is of vital significance, but when He repeats Himself even as He here does, we are being made to know just how serious all of this actually is.

Israel had lost her way and would now have to come under the yoke of Gentile powers, which God never intended. As such, she by and large lost her authority in the world, which, in fact, ultimately caused her total destruction. Even though the situation during the time of Ezekiel was very bad, still, the die was cast when Israel crucified Christ. Jesus said of her at that time, *"Your house is left unto you desolate"* (Mat. 23:38).

THE NEW COVENANT

Profaning the name of the Lord under the new covenant is far more subtle than it was under the old. And yet, in some sense of the word, it is almost identical.

As Israel of old lost sight of what the sacrifices actually meant, the modern church has long since forgotten what the cross actually means. So that makes the old and the new, at least in this capacity, one and the same. As Israel of old went into sin, likewise, the modern church does the same.

The basic difference is the idols. While the principle is the same, the type of idols is different now. Then it was heathenistic gods; now it centers up in self.

When the believer under the new covenant attempts to live for the Lord by means other than faith in Christ and what Christ did at the cross, in the eyes of God, such a believer has profaned the name of the Lord. In fact, the first four verses of Romans 7 proclaim such a person as living in spiritual adultery. Christ and the cross are to be looked to for everything, but when something is substituted in place of the cross, even though Jesus continues to be praised, the end result is always *"another Jesus"* (II Cor. 11:4).

Paul said that if we do such a thing, *"Christ shall profit you nothing"* (Gal. 5:2). In fact, the entirety of the epistle to the Galatians was written to address this very thing.

Israel was a nation; therefore, she went into bondage to the Gentile powers because of profaning the name of the Lord. The church is not a nation, but rather individual people, who are supposed to be born again. So the individual Christian doesn't come under the bondage of a nation, but rather of demon spirits (Gal. 5:1).

SANCTIFICATION

"And I will sanctify My great name, which was profaned among the heathen, which you have profaned in the midst of them; and the heathen shall know that I am the LORD, *says the* LORD GOD, *when I shall be sanctified in you before their eyes"* (Ezek. 36:23).

The Lord sanctified His great name when He sent His Son, the Lord Jesus Christ, to this world.

God's acts of grace toward guilty men solely because of His name as Saviour, and not because of any moral excellence in us, are shown in Ezekiel 36 (vv. 21, 22, 23, and 32). Therefore, the sinner's only claim for life and righteousness is his sinfulness and not his righteousness, of which he has none.

The phrase, *"When I shall be sanctified in you before their eyes,"* refers to the Lord's name always being set apart exclusively for sacred use.

The idea regarding their eyes is that due to Israel's sinfulness, Jehovah had been reduced to a feeble and local divinity.

The heathen had no understanding of Israel's disobedience, which resulted in their judgment. They merely thought that Jehovah was not strong or powerful enough to deliver, which in their eyes meant that their national gods were stronger than Jehovah.

CLEAN WATER

"For I will take you from among the heathen, and gather you out of all countries, and will bring you into your own land" (Ezek. 36:24).

The phrase, *"For I will take you from among the heathen … and will bring you into your own land,"* proclaims that which is not at all fulfilled, even at this time. Since 1948, Israel has been a state, which, of course, is a fulfillment of Bible prophecy, even this very verse. As a result, they have come from many countries of the world to make up modern Israel; however, as important and necessary as that is, this is not exactly that which was meant by the Holy Spirit.

It will be fulfilled in totality only at the second coming of Christ when Israel then accepts the Lord, as the next verse proclaims.

NO MORE FILTHINESS

"Then will I sprinkle clean water upon you, and you shall be clean: from all your filthiness, and from all your idols, will I cleanse you" (Ezek. 36:25).

By use of the word *then* in the phrase, *"Then will I sprinkle clean water upon you, and you shall be clean: from all your filthiness,"* it marks the time for the fulfillment of all these prophecies. Israel as a nation will not be won to Christ until the Antichrist is defeated by the second coming of Christ.

Israel, or any person for that matter, cannot be cleansed until they accept Christ as their Lord and Saviour. The Scripture plainly tells us, *"The blood of Jesus Christ His* (God's) *Son cleanses us from all sin"* (I Jn. 1:7). That is the only cleansing agent and, in fact, has always been the only cleansing agent.

HOW DOES THE BLOOD OF JESUS CHRIST CLEANSE FROM ALL SIN?

There is no cleansing agent per se in blood, as should be obvious. What is meant is this: When Jesus died on the cross, thereby, pouring out His life's blood and offering Himself in sacrifice, His life, as well as His physical body, was perfect in every respect. In other words, He was not born by natural procreation, but rather by decree of the Holy Spirit. Neither Joseph nor any other man was His father. In fact, Mary only provided a house for Him, so to speak, for the nine months of His being formed in His mother's womb. As a result, He didn't carry the traits of His mother or foster father, or His brothers and sisters. In fact, His conception and birth were totally unlike any conception and birth that had ever been. He was born without original sin, meaning that He had no sin nature. He was not a product of Adam's fall.

As well, His life was perfect and not tainted by sin in any respect, for He never sinned or failed in any respect—not in word, thought, or deed—which was done totally and completely for us. When He came to the end of His life and was ready to be offered, He said as it regarded evil, *"For the prince of this world comes, and has nothing in Me"* (Jn. 14:30).

So, when He died on the cross, He died as a perfect sacrifice. This was the pouring out of His life, which God did accept, and which atoned for all sin (Jn. 1:29). In fact, the Bible says that the life of the flesh is in the blood, so when Jesus poured out His precious blood, He was pouring out His life as a sacrifice.

Therefore, when the believing sinner accepts Christ as his Lord and Saviour and is instantly regenerated by the Holy Spirit, this is the born-again experience. All sin is atoned, spiritually speaking, and such a person is washed, sanctified, and justified *"in the name of the Lord Jesus, and by the Spirit of our God"* (I Cor. 6:11).

When any individual accepts Christ, the atoning work of Christ is accepted as well. This means that the sin debt, as it regards that particular individual, is totally erased and done away. It is no more chargeable to that person because Christ has paid the price. It is all done because of Him giving Himself on the cross and shedding His life's blood, which alone could effect our salvation.

POSSESSING THE DOUBLE

In ancient Israel they had a practice that was referred to as "possessing the double." The Scripture says concerning this,

"For your shame you shall have double; and for confusion they shall rejoice in their portion: therefore in their land they shall possess the double: everlasting joy shall be unto them" (Isa. 61:7).

Possessing the double pertained to the following: In ancient times, if someone in Israel went bankrupt, he was to list all of his indebtedness on a skin and have it posted in a conspicuous place for all to see. At times, a wealthy benefactor would come to the rescue and pay all the indebtedness. He would take down the skin and double it over, hence, hiding all of the indebtedness, and then write his name on the front. He would post it, as well, in a conspicuous place, and all could come to him for payment.

When Jesus died on the cross, He atoned for all sin. Upon faith in Him, He took down the list of all of our sins, doubled it over to where the sins could no longer be seen, and wrote His name on the front. This meant that all the indebtedness was settled. Therefore, every single believer in the world has the privilege of possessing the double.

THE NEW HEART AND THE NEW SPIRIT

"A new heart also will I give you, and a new spirit will I put within you: and I will take away the stony heart out of your flesh, and I will give you an heart of flesh" (Ezek. 36:26). This verse speaks of the new birth and totally refutes the claims of those who say that modern Israel will not be restored, and that they have no part or parcel in the gospel program presently or in the future.

These false teachers claim that this was offered to Israel through Christ but was rejected and, therefore, forfeited;

however, those claims do not match up with these promises. These promises proclaim a restoration, which means there will be no rejection or rebellion against Christ in that coming glad day. Of course, we are speaking of the coming kingdom age that will commence immediately after the second coming.

In other words, the prophecy is not conditional. Through foreknowledge the Lord proclaims what will be done because of what Israel will do in her acceptance of Christ, which is foretold not only by Ezekiel, but Isaiah, Jeremiah, Zechariah, and others.

THE SPIRIT OF THE LORD

"And I will put My Spirit within you, and cause you to walk in My statutes, and you shall keep My judgments, and do them" (Ezek. 36:27). This verse refers to the born-again experience but, as well, the baptism with the Holy Spirit. This speaks of the ratification of the new covenant given on the day of Pentecost (Acts 2:1–4). This, Israel could have had from the first advent of Christ if they had only accepted Him instead of rejecting Him.

Without the Holy Spirit, it is not possible to *"walk in My statutes, and ... keep My judgments"* (Acts 1:8; Rom. 8:11).

All of this corresponds exactly with that given in the New Testament of the regeneration of the individual soul (Jn. 3:3–8; Rom. 8:2, 5, 9; Gal. 5:22–23; Titus 3:5–6; I Pet. 1:22).

Regarding salvation, Israel must come in the same manner to Christ as any individual. They must accept Him by faith as all others do, and that they shall do after the second advent.

TWO KINDS OF SALVATION?

No!

Some have claimed that there are two kinds of salvation—one for the Jews and one for the Gentiles. This is error pure and simple because nowhere in the Bible is it taught that anyone can come to the Father except through Jesus Christ. Our Lord said, *"I am the way, the truth, and the life: no man comes unto the Father, but by Me"* (Jn. 14:6).

When Jesus said, *"No man,"* He meant exactly that.

Before the first advent of Christ, men were saved by looking forward to the price that would be paid at Calvary, of which the sacrifices of the lambs and bullocks were types. After the death and resurrection of Christ, men are saved by looking backward to Calvary and the price there paid. Concerning this very thing, Paul said:

> *Being justified freely by His grace* (made possible by the cross) *through the redemption that is in Christ Jesus* (carried out at the cross): *whom God has set forth to be a propitiation* (atonement or reconciliation or satisfaction) *through faith in His blood* (again, all of this is made possible by the cross), *to declare His righteousness for the remission of sins that are past* (refers to all who trusted Christ before He actually came, which covers the entirety of the time from the garden of Eden to the moment Jesus died on the cross), *through the forbearance* (tolerance) *of God* (meaning that God tolerated the situation before

Calvary, knowing the debt would be fully paid at that time) (Rom. 3:24-25).

There aren't two types of salvation, and, in fact, there never have been. From the time the Lord killed an animal and made coats of skins and clothed Adam and Eve, which replaced their fig leaves, the way of salvation—Christ and Him crucified—was plainly marked and has never changed and will never change (Gen. 3:21; Gen. 4).

THE CROSS

Satan's greatest effort has always been to subtly set Calvary aside as the answer to man's dilemma. He has been amazingly successful. In Paul's day men attempted to add to the finished work of Christ by claiming that in order to be saved, one had to accept Christ plus keep the law (Acts 15:1).

Unfortunately, Satan's efforts did not end with the early church. Actually, the early church began to apostatize after the death of the apostle Paul and the apostles of Christ and those who knew them. By the third century, the leaven of works religion was insidiously making its way into the church.

By the sixth century AD, the church had so apostatized until it was well on its way to becoming the Catholic Church, which is purely a man-made institution. It is no less today. Sadly, much of the Protestant church follows the same path of salvation by works.

Paul said that if works are inserted into that which is to be solely of faith, one has *"fallen from grace"* (Gal. 5:4). In other words, one cannot trust in works and faith at the same time. When we say "faith," we are speaking of the correct object of faith, which must be Christ, and Him crucified (I Cor. 1:17-18, 21, 23; 2:2; Col. 2:10-15; Gal. 6:14).

Actually, this is what caused Israel to lose her way. Paul said, *"For they being ignorant of God's righteousness, and going about to establish their own righteousness, have not submitted themselves unto the righteousness of God"* (Rom. 10:3).

THE GREED MESSAGE

At the present time, Satan's greatest effort against God's true plan of salvation is the greed message, which is the primary message of the so-called Word of Faith doctrine.

This erroneous message, which has made great inroads into Pentecostal and charismatic churches, is very subtly presented and, thereby, very easily deceives its many followers. It is a heady doctrine because it appeals to greed and pride, which has always been Satan's chief approach (Gen. 3:4–5).

Inasmuch as Scripture is used but subtly twisted in order to sponsor this doctrine, many are deceived. Satan's prime efforts are always cloaked in a heavy panoply of religion; consequently, Israel would kill the Lord in the name of the Lord.

The greed message subtly sets aside man's real problem, which is sin, and the solution, which is Christ and Him crucified, and instead, promotes material blessings and benefits. In the preaching of this message, which Paul called *"another gospel,"* the blood of Jesus Christ is subtly, cunningly, and quietly set aside.

Most of the advocates of this spurious doctrine (and spurious it is) would deny what is being said here; however, if one is to notice, the emphasis, at least for the most part, is not on Christ and Him crucified, but instead, on material prosperity.

Inasmuch as there is some truth in this error, as there is some truth in most all error, it easily deceives and, thereby, attracts many followers. As stated, money and pride have great appeal.

ANOTHER GOSPEL

In fact, most of the preaching presently is little lifting up Christ and Him crucified as the answer to man's dilemma. It is given lip service, if at all. The church is busy trying to save society instead of saving men out of society, which is the true purpose of Christ. The Bible teaches that society is evil, corrupt, and, thereby, doomed. Trying to improve society is like trying to improve self. It cannot be done. To be frank, the self-improvement gospel is presently the greatest effort of all. It appeals to the flesh because it appeals to man's pride. Man likes to think that he can correct his problems of emotional disturbances, wrong direction, lack of confidence, etc., all by correcting self. The pulpits are full of this type of message, which, in fact, doesn't recognize man's true problem, which is sin, and the true solution, and I might quickly add the only solution, which is Jesus Christ and Him crucified.

Paul said, *"I determined not to know anything among you, save Jesus Christ, and Him crucified"* (I Cor. 2:2). He said this because man's problem is sin and because the only solution to sin is what Christ did at Calvary. Consequently, any church that is not a cross church is not a true church of Jesus Christ. As well, if the church goes beyond the cross, it always goes into heresy.

REGENERATION

"And you shall dwell in the land that I gave to your fathers; and you shall be My people, and I will be your God" (Ezek. 36:28). This verse says three things:

1. Israel will dwell in the land that God gave to their fathers.
2. Israel will be God's people as was originally intended.
3. The Lord will be their God and not idols, etc.

All of this tells us that the land of Israel is not like any other country in the world. Its biblical boundaries are protected by the Lord, and within those boundaries, the people of Israel, i.e., the Israelis, there should dwell.

It does not belong to the Palestinians, to the Muslims, or anyone else for that matter.

In 1948, when President Truman placed the power and prestige of America behind the formation of the state of Israel, it was to be according to biblical boundaries, and it was to be given the biblical name of Israel, and thus it was. To be sure, God will bless or judge the countries of this world that deal with Israel. If dealt with in a negative way, they will one day answer to God, and if dealt with in a positive way, they will be blessed by God.

THE NEW MAN

"I will also save you from all your uncleannesses: and I will call for the corn, and will increase it, and lay no famine upon you" (Ezek. 36:29).

In actuality, the phrase, *"I will also save you from all your uncleannesses,"* should be the last phrase of Ezekiel 36:28.

As it regards salvation, regeneration and not reformation—a new heart and not a changed heart—is that which must be.

The Holy Spirit never attempts to change the old man, but instead, makes a new man (Rom. 6:6–7; II Cor. 5:17; Gal. 6:15).

If the word *change* is used in the sense of changing from one form to a new form, as in the resurrection (I Cor. 15:51), then the use is scriptural and, thereby, legitimate.

The great theme of the world is rehabilitation; however, the word is not found in the Bible, and for the simple reason that God does not rehabilitate anyone. He makes a new creation. It's called *"born again"* (Jn. 3:3). In other words, as previously stated, it is a new heart and not a changed heart. It is not the changing of the old man, but rather the making of a new man.

INCREASE

"And I will multiply the fruit of the tree, and the increase of the field, that you shall receive no more reproach of famine among the heathen" (Ezek. 36:30). This verse means that in that coming glad day, and we speak of the coming kingdom age when Israel will have accepted Jesus Christ as their Messiah, Saviour, and Lord,

Israel at that time will be abundantly blessed in every capacity. It will be so much, in fact, that Israel at that time will be the foremost nation in the world, but only after they have accepted Jesus Christ, who alone can make a new man. In the making of this new man, he will then make a new Israel. In a sense, at that time they will be the priestly nation of the world.

REPENTANCE

"Then shall you remember your own evil ways, and your doings that were not good, and shall loathe yourselves in your own sight for your iniquities and for your abominations" (Ezek. 36:31).

This new moral nature will be a gift to Israel of the sovereignty of God, but Israel will ask for it, for this responsibility will attach to them. Sovereign grace and human responsibility are coexistent (Phil. 2:12–13). In fact, the effect of grace is self-judgment.

Tyre and Assyria claimed to be like the garden of Eden, but the similitude belongs only to Israel (Ezek. 28:13; 31:8–9).

The theme of these chapters is the relationship between Jehovah and His people; hence, there are no details given respecting the first advent. The phrase of Ezekiel 36:31, *"Then shall you remember your own evil ways,"* proclaims the fact that the effect of grace is always self-judgment.

THE GRACE OF GOD

This is so important that I felt that I had to say it again. When men attempt to earn their salvation by works, as do most, they never really see their own evil ways. Such can only be seen when we properly see the cross. Then and then only do we see Christ, and seeing Christ puts ourselves in proper perspective, with self then losing its attractiveness.

True Bible repentance demands that the individual sees himself as God sees him. Paul called it *"godly sorrow,"* which *"works repentance to salvation not to be repented of,"* i.e. will not be sorry that he has repented (II Cor. 7:10). A corrupt church attempts to build self-esteem, while the Holy Spirit attempts to destroy self-esteem, with self being lost in Christ. The answer is as Paul said, *"For you are dead, and your life is hid with Christ in God"* (Col. 3:3).

THE MERCY OF GOD

"Not for your sakes do I this, says the Lord GOD, be it known unto you: be ashamed and confounded for your own ways, O house of Israel" (Ezek. 36:32). The phrase, *"Not for your sakes do I this, says the Lord GOD,"* goes not only for Israel but, as well, for all of humanity.

Actually, there was no way that the Lord could do such for their sakes, or for our sakes for that matter, simply because they, as well as we, lack any merit at all. All that is done for the child of God is done *"for Christ's sake"* (Eph. 4:32; I Jn. 2:12).

Actually, to get down to the bedrock, all of this can take place within our hearts and lives, which is the greatest blessing of all, but only if we understand the cross of Christ as it regards not only salvation, but sanctification as well. Salvation is justification by faith, while sanctification could also be called "sanctification by faith." The sad fact is that the modern church has some inkling of knowledge regarding justification by faith but none at all as it regards sanctification by faith. As a result, those in the modern church, at least those who truly love the Lord, consistently try to sanctify themselves, which is impossible.

THE OVERCOMER

Let me give you an example: Some seven times in Revelation 2 and 3, the Lord tells the believer that he must be an overcomer. The question is, how do we do that? The truth is, we cannot do it of ourselves. It is impossible. We can do it God's way, and then it will be done. But what is that way?

First of all, we are to understand that we are already overcomers, that is, if our faith is in Christ and what Christ has done for us at the cross. The problem we have is that we're trying to overcome certain things in our lives, thinking that then we will be overcomers, which we are never able to do.

We must understand the following: As stated, we are already overcomers, meaning that at this very moment, we are overcomers, that is, if our faith is in Christ and His finished work. With our faith being properly placed and maintained, then we will begin to see these problems drop off one by one. If we try to do it ourselves, it never gets done simply because it's impossible.

And yet, it's very difficult for us to think to ourselves that we are overcomers now. We see the problems, the weaknesses, the faults, and the failures, and we wonder how that we can claim to be overcomers with all of these things staring at us in the face.

We are overcomers simply because Jesus Christ is an overcomer, and we are in Him (Jn. 14:20). We keep trying to do it ourselves, and this is something we cannot do. Yet, Christ has already done this thing for us, and it only requires faith on our part, but it must be faith in Christ and His finished work (Rom. 6:1-14; 8:1-11; I Cor. 1:17-18, 23; 2:2; Gal. 6:14; Col. 2:10-15).

BLESSING

"Thus says the Lord GOD; In the day that I shall have cleansed you from all your iniquities I will also cause you to dwell in the cities, and the wastes shall be built" (Ezek. 36:33). The phrase, *"And the wastes shall be built,"* proclaims the fact that Israel's conversion to Christ will precipitate their blessing. Only when all iniquities have been cleansed can the individual then dwell in the inheritance, with the wastes then being reclaimed, i.e., built.

If believers will truly live for God with all of their strength, heart, and soul, and will believe God for blessings, those blessings will definitely come.

Believers should expect the Lord to bless them, and such blessing will come in every stripe. Let's look at what the Lord said that He would do:

- *"And all these blessings shall come on you, and overtake you"* (Deut. 28:2).
- *"The LORD shall command the blessing upon you in your storehouses, and in all that you set your hand unto"* (Deut. 28:8).

- *"And the* LORD *shall make you plentiful in goods"* (Deut. 28:11).
- *"The* LORD *shall open unto you His good treasure"* (Deut. 28:12).
- *"And the* LORD *shall make you the head, and not the tail"* (Deut. 28:13).

Some would read these tremendous promises and state, "Brother Swaggart, that's in the Old Testament, and it doesn't apply to us today." Nothing could be further from the truth.

In fact, anything and everything the Lord promised His people in the Old Testament (under the old covenant), He will do much more under the new covenant. Concerning this very thing, Paul said:

> *But now* (since the cross) *has He* (the Lord Jesus) *obtained a more excellent ministry* (the new covenant in Jesus' blood is superior and takes the place of the old covenant in animal blood), *but how much also He is the mediator of a better covenant* (proclaims the fact that Christ officiates between God and man according to the arrangements of the new covenant), *which was established upon better promises.* (This presents the new covenant explicitly based on the cleansing and forgiveness of all sin, which the old covenant could never do) (Heb. 8:6).

So we are told here that we now have a better covenant based on better promises, meaning that whatever the Lord promised under the old covenant, He will do even much more under the new covenant. As a believer, you must believe that and act upon that. Anticipate God's blessings! Look forward to His blessings! He loves faith, and above all, faith in His finished work.

NO MORE DESOLATION

"And the desolate land shall be tilled, whereas it lay desolate in the sight of all who passed by" (Ezek. 36:34). As all of this applies to Israel, let it be understood that it applies to us as well. The phrase, *"And the desolate land shall be tilled,"* proclaims the fact that the land of Israel will be blessed as well as its people.

In fact, the people must be blessed first before the land can be blessed. Israel getting right with God will bring about the desolate land being changed. And, as previously stated, that goes for every believer now.

THE GARDEN OF EDEN

"And they shall say, This land that was desolate is become like the garden of Eden; and the waste and desolate and ruined cities are become fenced, and are inhabited" (Ezek. 36:35). The phrase, *"Like the garden of Eden,"* proclaims what this land will be. Regarding that coming glad day, if the Holy Spirit refers to Israel as the garden of Eden, then it should be obvious that the beauty of such will be beyond imagination.

In the spiritual sense, this is what can happen in the heart and life of every believer and, in fact, is what is meant to happen. The Lord desires to make a garden of Eden out of our life and living. It can only be done as the believer firmly looks to Christ and the cross, understanding that what is needed can only be brought about by the sacrifice of Christ and our faith in that finished work.

As stated, the world keeps trying to improve self, but it can only somewhat decorate the exterior, but even that fades, and fast. It is sadder yet when the church has bought into this message of self-improvement, which it definitely has in the last few years. But an improvement of self is not man's need.

Outside of Christ, and that goes for the believer who is not looking solely to Christ and the cross, self is ugly, corrupt, ungodly, filthy, and wicked. I realize that's strong, but, in fact, it's not strong enough.

Self, at least if it is to be what it ought to be, can only be made aright by being placed firmly in Christ, which can only be done by looking to the cross. Let us say it one more time:

- The only way to God is through Christ (Jn. 14:6).
- The only way to Christ is through the cross (I Cor. 1:17–18, 23).
- The only way to the cross is through a denial of self (Lk. 9:23–24).

THE LORD

"Then the heathen who are left round about you shall know that I the LORD *build the ruined places, and plant that that was desolate: I the* LORD *have spoken it, and I will do it"* (Ezek. 36:36). This verse proclaims the fact that the name of the Lord must

be glorified in the earth, which it most definitely will be at the time of the coming kingdom age.

At that time, the entirety of the world will know that Jesus is the Son of God, that He is the Saviour of mankind, and that He effected salvation by and through what He did at the cross.

Then, there will be no more Islam, Hinduism, Catholicism, Buddhism, etc. As well, all forms of Christianity that have been corrupted will fall by the wayside. There will be nothing left but Christ, and He will rule personally from Jerusalem, and the *"government shall be upon His shoulder"* (Isa. 9:6).

THE INCREASE

"Thus says the Lord GOD; *I will yet for this be enquired of by the house of Israel, to do it for them; I will increase them with men like a flock"* (Ezek. 36:37). This verse refers to the coming great tribulation of the future, which will bring Israel to utter desolation and even threatened annihilation, which will precipitate their crying to God for deliverance. This will bring them to a full repentance and dependence on the Lord (Isa. 64; Zech. 12:10; 13:1; Mat. 23:37–39; Rom. 11:25–29).

Sometimes the Lord has to resort to stringent measures before certain people will heed. Perhaps that's true for all of us. The idea is that Israel will definitely be brought to a place of full repentance and dependence upon the Lord. It won't come easily, but it will come.

In fact, that's the main reason for the great tribulation. It is to bring Israel back to God.

THE HOLY FLOCK

"As the holy flock, as the flock of Jerusalem in her solemn feasts; so shall the waste cities be filled with flocks of men: and they shall know that I am the Lord*"* (Ezek. 36:38). The phrase, *"So shall the waste cities be filled with flocks of men,"* proclaims this earthly glory and blessing. This will, as well, trigger the blessing of all the other nations of the world. Even though it is little known, the prosperity of the world hinges on Israel's prosperity. This prosperity is all anchored in Christ and cannot be brought about until Christ is recognized and accepted.

However, it shall happen because the Lord has spoken it, and He will do it.

The moment a sinner believes,
And trusts in his crucified Lord,
His pardon at once he receives
Redemption in full through His blood.
The faith that unites to the Lamb,
And brings such salvation as this,
Is more than mere fancy, or name
The work of God's Spirit it is.

It treads on the world and on hell,
It vanquishes death and despair;
And what is still stranger to tell
It overcomes heaven by prayer
Permits a vile worm of the dust,
With God to commune as a friend;
His promise of mercy to trust,
And look for His love to the end.

It says to the mountains, Depart,
That stand between God and the soul;
It binds up the broken in heart,
The wounded in spirit makes whole;
Bids sins of a crimson-like dye,
Be spotless as snow, and as white;
And raises the sinner on high,
To dwell with the angels of life.

CHAPTER 3

THE HAND OF
THE LORD

THE HAND OF THE LORD

"THE HAND OF THE LORD was upon me, and carried me out in the Spirit of the Lord, and set me down in the midst of the valley which was full of bones" (Ezek. 37:1).

PROPHECY UPON THESE BONES

The first prophecy of Ezekiel 37 (vv. 1–14) foretells the moral, national, and physical resurrection of Israel; the second prophecy (Ezekiel 37:15–28) predicts the unity of the nation and its happy settlement in the land of Israel under the government of the Messiah.[1]

We will find that the repetition of the word *behold* fastens the attention upon two facts: the bones were very many and very dry.

Williams said, "The commanding voice of Cyrus raised the exiles out of their captivity grave and restored them to the land of Israel; however, that voice is not the voice of this chapter.

The voice of this chapter will be altogether mightier, and will raise the nation from its present long-continued dispersion and moral death, to the position of the greatest in the world. This will take place at the coming kingdom age."[2]

THE VALLEY OF DRY BONES

As the last chapter graphically spoke of Israel's coming restoration, Ezekiel, Chapter 37, graphically portrays the spiritual manner of that restoration.

It has been approximately 2,500 years since the prophet had this vision, and it is just now coming to pass, but it will not be completed until the second coming of the Lord. As well, between now and that particular time, Israel is going to face its darkest days yet. However, despite those coming darkened days, which Jesus said would be worse than any that had ever been or ever would be, these prophecies, down to the minutest detail, will be fulfilled (Mat. 24:21–22).

Most of Ezekiel's prophecies begin with the word *and*, *also*, or *moreover*; however, these customary words are missing in this particular prophecy, indicating something extraordinary, which is obvious.

THE SPIRIT OF THE LORD

In Ezekiel 37:1, the phrase, *"In the Spirit of the LORD,"* indicates that this was a vision and that Ezekiel was not literally taken to this valley, etc.

The phrase, *"And set me down in the midst of the valley which was full of bones,"* indicates the spiritual and national identity of Israel as being dead.

Even the most rudimentary Bible student would have to recognize the truth of the destiny of these people called Jews or Israelis. If one knows anything at all about their history, one knows that their survival has been an absolute impossibility except for God. Their entire history is one of conflict and persecution, coupled with a sheer determination to remain alive.

Someone has said that the Jew is God's prophetic time clock, and so they are. The only way that these people could have survived through the centuries (and especially now) as a distinct nation in their own land is that God has kept them alive for a purpose. That purpose is twofold:

1. To keep the promises that He made to the patriarchs and the prophets (Gen. 12:1–3; II Sam. 7:16).
2. Israel's restoration will signal the blessings of all the nations of the world under Christ (Ps. 67).

When Judah fell to the Babylonian invader, Jehovah took the scepter of power from the hands of the kings of Judah and placed it in the hands of the Gentiles. It has remained there ever since, called by Christ *"the times of the Gentiles"* (Lk. 21:24).

THE RESTORATION OF ISRAEL

Upon the second coming of the Lord and Israel's acceptance of Christ as Lord and Messiah, the times of the Gentiles will come to a close, with Israel once again assuming the role of world leadership under Christ. This is a position that she would not have lost except for sin, but she will then be restored, as this chapter and so many others proclaim.

The world little knows or understands that the prosperity of all the nations of the world hinges on these people. Consequently, even though they are now spiritually dead and have been for a long, long time, still, God will bless the nation that blesses Israel and curse the nation that curses Israel (Gen. 12:1–3).

When Israel became a nation in 1948, which was the beginning of the fulfillment of this very chapter, England opposed her effort strongly. From that day until this, England's power has waned and weakened around the world until she is only a shell of her former self. Much of this deterioration can be laid at the doorstep of her opposition to these ancient people and the prophecies being fulfilled. To oppose that which belongs to God, irrespective of its present spiritual condition, is to oppose God. It is a position in which no man, nation, or kingdom desires to be.

Conversely, the United States strongly aided and abetted Israel in her formation as a nation and her sustenance since.

Shortly before his death, President Harry S. Truman was asked what he considered to be his most important contribution as the holder of the highest office in the land. The president quickly replied, "Helping Israel become a nation." His answer shocked the reporter.

In the evening of his life, spiritual matters became very real to President Truman, and evidently the Lord revealed to him the spiritual and political significance of this act.

The only answer to the survival of the Jew and the national identity of the nation of Israel is God. There is no other answer, as there can be no other answer.

THEY WERE VERY DRY

"And caused me to pass by them round about: and, behold, there were very many in the open valley; and, lo, they were very dry" (Ezek. 37:2). This verse speaks of a total absence of spirituality. In other words, what is even now happening to Israel is not because of any spirituality on their part, when, in fact, there is none at all, but it rather signifies that the work is strictly at the behest of the Lord.

They are *"very dry"* as a result of having rejected their Messiah and even crucified Him. They have survived the centuries and become a nation in 1948 because of the hand of God at work. In fact, it is 100 percent because of God working on their behalf.

Even now, there is not an ounce of spirituality in the land of Israel. In fact, many Jews are atheistic or agnostic.

Even the few who claim to believe the Old Testament are bogged down in legalism and incorrect interpretations of the Bible. Paul said, *"Blindness in part is happened to Israel, until the fulness of the Gentiles be come in"* (Rom. 11:25). That blindness is no less now than it was then, if not deeper.

However, concerning this very narrative and regarding the conclusion of the times of the Gentiles, Paul also said that *"all Israel shall be saved"* (Rom. 11:26).

CAN THESE BONES LIVE?

"And He said unto me, Son of man, can these bones live? And I answered, O Lord GOD, You know" (Ezek. 37:3). This verse actually proclaims the impossibility of such a thing, at least as far as human beings are concerned.

An American general was viewing the horror of the Nazi death camps in 1945, where some 6 million Jews were murdered by Hitler and his henchmen. Upon seeing the thousands of dead bodies and the thousands who were near death, he said that this very passage came to him at that moment—*"Can these bones live?"*

In answer to that question, in 1948, when Israel once again became a nation after nearly 2,000 years, the prophecy began to be fulfilled.

Ezekiel's answer to the question of the Lord, *"O Lord GOD, You know,"* signifies that the task within the realm of human endeavor was impossible. If they, in fact, were made to *"live,"* it would have to be done by the hand of God.

Inasmuch as this prophecy was given shortly after the fall of Judah and Jerusalem, Ezekiel's mind had to have been filled with these recent events. Whether at that time he was able to look beyond that moment to a future day so very, very far away, one can only guess. However, once the vision of the restoration of the land and the graphic design of the temple were given to him, as is outlined in Ezekiel 40-48, more than likely his understanding of that future day was greatly increased.

PROPHESY

"Again He said unto me, Prophesy upon these bones, and say unto them, O you dry bones, hear the word of the Lord," (Ezek. 37:4). This verse proclaims the fact that the Lord will give a word that will guarantee their restoration and revival; however, such would only be done according to the word of the Lord.

As an aside, many have taken this passage out of context, thinking they can prophesy things into existence according to their own liking, direction, or will; however, such can be only if it is the will of God. Therefore, the intimation seems to be that if it is God's will concerning a particular situation, irrespective of how personal or impersonal it may be, according to the word of the Lord, one can prophesy upon the situation, and it will hasten its success. However, it is only the word of the Lord that has the power to bring about the miraculous. When one considers that these words that were uttered some 2,500 years ago are now beginning to be fulfilled before our very eyes, one is made to understand the absolute power of the Word of God.

BREATH

"Thus saith the Lord God unto these bones; Behold, I will cause breath to enter into you, and ye shall live" (Ezek. 37:5). The *"breath"* mentioned in this verse has the same meaning as Genesis 2:7. The breath spoken of is the same breath that God *"breathed into his nostrils the breath of life,"* respecting Adam, and he became *"a living soul."*

The life that is spoken of in this passage speaks of national life and spiritual life. The national life has already begun, with Israel having become a nation once again in 1948 and continuing. However, the spiritual life will begin in the coming great tribulation when 144,000 Jews will accept Christ as their Saviour, with, no doubt, others accepting the Lord, as well, after that event. (Rev. 7). Nevertheless, the fullness of spiritual life will not come until the second coming (Zech. 13:1, 9).

As the Spirit of God is the only one who can breathe life into unregenerate man who is dead in trespasses and sins, likewise, He is the only one who can bring Israel back. To be sure, the Spirit of God, who moved upon the face of a ruined and formless world (Gen. 1:2), will move upon ruined and formless Israel and, in fact, has already begun to do so.

Ezekiel would later say regarding his vision of the coming temple (we speak of the millennial temple) and the river (a type of the Holy Spirit), which will flow out from under the threshold of that house, that *"everything shall live whither the river comes"* (Ezek. 47:1, 9).

As well, to every weary heart, to every thirsty soul, and to everyone who longs for righteousness, the Lord is saying the same to you that He said of old concerning Israel, *"I will cause breath to enter into you, and you shall live"* (Ezek. 37:5).

I AM THE LORD

"And I will lay sinews upon you, and will bring up flesh upon you, and cover you with skin, and put breath in you, and you

shall live; and you shall know that I am the LORD*"* (Ezek. 37:6). Even though this verse is the Lord is speaking of Israel, as an aside, it proclaims to us the secret of how the Lord originally made man (Gen. 2:7).

As stated, this has already begun regarding Israel's national identity, but it will not begin spiritually until the great tribulation, and more specifically, at the second coming of the Lord.

Actually, Ezekiel 37:6 specifically speaks of Israel's national and spiritual identity.

The national identity, which has already begun, speaks of the reconstruction of the external skeleton by bringing together its different parts and clothing them with sinews, flesh, and skin.

However, the second stage, which is the spiritual identity, will not be brought about until He breathes spiritual life into them.

If, in fact, the first part is already being fulfilled (and it definitely is), this means that we are very close to the second stage being fulfilled. Therefore, how close is the church to the rapture?

On July 1, 1985, at about 9 a.m. on a Monday morning, the Lord gave me a vision of the world harvest and the coming storm. In the vision I saw the heavens that were boiling in blackness as I had never seen before, and it was coming out of the east. The Lord told me that He would delay the storm for a short period of time until the harvest could be gathered.

Even though the Lord did not specifically say such to me, I believe the vision of the storm, coupled with the fields ready to harvest, signified the coming great and terrible tribulation period.

As we look at these prophecies and even the beginning stages of their fulfillment, we know that we're living in the last of the last days.

THE BONES CAME TOGETHER

"So I prophesied as I was commanded: and as I prophesied, there was a noise, and behold a shaking, and the bones came together, bone to his bone" (Ezek. 37:7).

The phrase, *"And as I prophesied, there was a noise,"* in the Hebrew actually means "a voice." So this noise—a voice—could have actually been the voice of the archangel with the *shaking* speaking of the resurrection, signifying the rapture of the church.

Actually, Israel will come into full flower at the outset of the great tribulation. She will think that the Antichrist is the Messiah, which will signify the bones coming together even in a greater way; however, as the next verse suggests, the Antichrist is not the Messiah and, therefore, can breathe no breath of life into them but, in fact, will only bring death.

NO BREATH

"And when I beheld, lo, the sinews and the flesh came up upon them, and the skin covered them above: but there was no breath in them" (Ezek. 37:8). The phrase of this verse, *"But there was no breath in them,"* concerns their national identity but definitely not their spiritual identity.

In fact, Israel will accept the Man of Sin as the Messiah, as prophesied by Christ when He said, *"I am come in My Father's name, and you receive Me not: if another shall come in his own name, him you will receive"* (Jn. 5:43).

The false one whom Israel will receive is the *"another"* spoken of by Christ. As the false messiah, he can give no breath of life. Only Christ, the true Messiah, can do that.

Actually, as a result of their deception, in the latter half of the great tribulation, they will come close to annihilation, with the Antichrist turning on them and seeking to destroy them as a people and a nation.

At this time, according to the prophet Zechariah, two-thirds will die (Zech. 13:8–9).

PROPHESY UNTO THE SPIRIT

"Then said He unto me, Prophesy unto the wind, prophesy, son of man, and say to the wind, Thus says the Lord GOD; *Come from the four winds, O breath, and breathe upon these slain, that they may live"* (Ezek. 37:9). The phrase, *"Then said He unto me, Prophesy unto the wind,"* actually says in the Hebrew, *"Prophesy unto the Spirit."* The phrase, *"Come from the four winds,"* actually says in the Hebrew, *"Come from the four breaths."*

The number four is symbolic of fourfold, denoting an absolute, total, and complete restoration.

The phrase, *"And breathe upon these slain, that they may live,"* denotes the truth that in the mind of God, for all practical and spiritual purposes, Israel is dead.

The word *prophesy* denotes the Word of the Lord, which means that it is "forever settled in heaven" and cannot be denied, and neither can it fail.

Doubt and unbelief would think it absurd prophesying over these bones; however, faith says, *"They shall live."*

SPIRITUAL LIFE

"So I prophesied as He commanded me, and the breath came into them, and they lived, and stood up upon their feet, an exceeding great army" (Ezek. 37:10). This verse now speaks of Israel's spiritual identity, signifying their spiritual revival, which will take place at the second coming.

The phrase, *"And stood upon their feet,"* pertains to the action part of the spiritual life, which enables such to be done.

For a long time, even over 2,000 years, Israel has not stood upon their feet spiritually. In the coming glad day, they shall! Then they shall be an exceeding great army, but it will be an exceeding great army for the Lord.

So, we have had the national identity, and now we have the spiritual identity; however, the latter cannot be brought about until Jesus Christ was and is accepted, which He most definitely shall be.

THE THIRTEEN TRIBES

"Then He said unto me, Son of man, these bones are the whole house of Israel: behold, they say, Our bones are dried, and our hope

is lost: we are cut off for our parts" (Ezek. 37:11). The phrase, *"The whole house of Israel,"* speaks of the entirety of the 13 tribes, and the fact that they will no more be divided but whole.

The latter part of this verse, speaking of Israel's exclamation, *"Behold, they say,"* refers to the latter half of the coming great tribulation. At that time it will look as though the entirety of their nation will be totally destroyed, with hope lost and *"cut off for our parts."* This has reference to Zechariah's prophecy when he said, *"Two parts therein shall be cut off and die"* (Zech. 13:8).

At that time they will be at the conclusion of the second half of the great tribulation. Three and one-half years before, they will have suffered a terrible defeat at the hands of the Antichrist, with him taking over Jerusalem and threatening the very existence of these ancient people.

In the battle of Armageddon, as Ezekiel will describe in Ezekiel 38 and 39, and as Zechariah prophesied, it will look as if all *"hope is lost."* Actually, all hope would be lost but for the coming of the Lord; however, He will come, and, as well, He will have *"healing in His wings"* (Mal. 4:2–3).

GRAVES

"Therefore prophesy and say unto them, Thus says the Lord GOD; Behold, O My people, I will open your graves, and cause you to come up out of your graves, and bring you into the land of Israel" (Ezek. 37:12). This verse pertains to a double fulfillment.

As prophecy sometimes does, the previous verse spoke of the last few months, or even weeks, before the coming of the

Lord and, therefore, the relief of Israel, whereas, this verse goes back even to World War II and forward.

Even though this verse is symbolic of Israel's destitute spiritual condition, it also is literal.

At the end of World War II, with 6 million Jews slaughtered by Hitler, the Jews became a cohesive nation some three years later. Then literally began the fulfillment of this passage and *"cause you to come up out of your graves, and bring you into the land of Israel."*

Since that time, hundreds of thousands of Jews have come from all over the world, immigrating to the land of Israel, with the latest excursion from the former Soviet Union not being the least.

As well, the fulfillment of this passage concerning the second development will take place after the coming of the Lord when every Jew on the face of the earth will be brought to the land of Israel (Isa. 11:11–12; 56:8).

AND YOU SHALL KNOW THAT I AM THE LORD

"And you shall know that I am the LORD, when I have opened your graves, O My people, and brought you up out of your graves" (Ezek. 37:13). This verse proclaims that which Israel does not yet know; however, this they will know at the second coming.

The phrase, *"And brought you up out of your graves,"* has reference to the fact that for all practical purposes, in the battle of Armageddon, Israel is all but totally destroyed. Actually, there is no earthly way they can be salvaged; however, there is a heavenly way, and that heavenly way is Christ!

THE HOLY SPIRIT

"And shall put My Spirit in you, and you shall live, and I shall place you in your own land: then shall you know that I the LORD have spoken it, and performed it, says the LORD" (Ezek. 37:14). This verse signifies the great revival that will take place in Israel at the coming of the Lord. Zechariah gave more detail on the happening of this great moving of the Holy Spirit (Zech. 12:10–14; 13:1, 9).

This will actually be the greatest revival or restoration the world has ever known. Almost all Jews, if not all, will accept Christ as their own personal Saviour and will recognize Him at long last as the Messiah.

The formula, "Says Jehovah," is to be understood as a confirmation written at the foot of the prophecy, saying, "This is Jehovah's declaration."

THE SECOND PROPHECY

"The word of the LORD came again unto me, saying" (Ezek. 37:15).

The second prophecy of this chapter, which begins with Ezekiel 37:15, predicts the future union of the tribes, their restoration to the land of Israel, and their settlement there under one shepherd. It teaches that a divinely wrought union is real and enduring; it brings its subjects into fellowship with God; and it disposes them around a divine center, who and which is Christ.

As the first restoration from Babylon was opposed by Satan, so will he oppose Israel's future settlement in the land of Israel, which he is doing presently. The time frame, however, of the great opposition will be the latter half of the great tribulation. The two following chapters deal with this and foretell the agents Satan will employ. Actually, this which Ezekiel gives us destroys the Anglo-Israelite theory, i.e., that the United States and Great Britain are the two lost tribes of Israel.

THE TWO STICKS

"Moreover, you son of man, take you one stick, and write upon it, For Judah, and for the children of Israel his companions: then take another stick, and write upon it, For Joseph, the stick of Ephraim and for all the house of Israel his companions" (Ezek. 37:16).

The two sticks of this verse represent the two houses of Israel—the northern confederation of Israel sometimes called Ephraim or Samaria and the southern kingdom known as Judah.

It is amazing that God would use something so simple as two sticks to emphasize something that is of such great significance. However, we must understand that the Lord doesn't care what people think. He will do whatever it is He desires to prove His point.

JOIN THEM TOGETHER

"And join them one to another into one stick; and they shall become one in your hand" (Ezek. 37:17). This verse predicts that

both sticks (both kingdoms) will now become one stick, i.e., signifying one people, which will be brought about by the hand of the Lord and will never again be divided. In fact, the division was never of the Lord but was brought about because of sin.

Under both David and Solomon, the land was one, but with the death of Solomon, the nation divided, with some nine tribes making up the northern kingdom and Judah and Benjamin making up the southern kingdom. Levi and Simeon were added to Judah because Simeon's inheritance was within the inheritance of Judah (Josh. 19:1).

WHAT DO YOU MEAN?

"And when the children of your people shall speak unto you, saying, Will you not show us what you mean by these?" (Ezek. 37:18).

The division remained for about 260 years until the northern kingdom of Israel was taken into captivity by the Assyrians, where it remained, leaving only the southern kingdom of Judah.

Judah lasted for approximately 133 years after Israel's fall before falling to the Babylonians, again, all because of sin.

After the dispersion of some 70 years, parts of the entirety of the 13 tribes came back into the land and formed one nation, as they were upon the birth of Christ.

ONE IN MY HAND

"Say unto them, Thus says the Lord GOD; Behold, I will take the stick of Joseph, which is in the hand of Ephraim, and the tribes of

Israel his fellows, and will put them with him, even with the stick of Judah, and make them one stick, and they shall be one in My hand" (Ezek. 37:19). This verse proclaims the bringing of these people back together as the Lord always intended.

The cause was an unlawful breaking off from the house of Judah and the establishment of an independent kingdom. The house of Joseph actually said, *"What portion have we in David? and we have none inheritance in the son of Jesse"* (II Chron. 10:16).

At that time the northern kingdom forsook all that the covenant stood for, which promised a coming Redeemer, i.e., inheritance.

While in a sense this began in 1948, it will not come to a completion until the second coming of the Lord when Israel will then accept Christ not only as her Saviour but, as well, as her Messiah. It is amazing that the prophet Ezekiel could proclaim these things some 2,500 years ago. Actually, when Israel became a nation once again in 1948, and that after some 2,000 years of being scattered all over the world, such had never happened before in human history. So, the very state of Israel is a fulfillment of Bible prophecy and something that is so stupendous as to beggar description, and yet, the world pays no attention to it whatsoever.

WHAT WERE THESE STICKS?

"And the sticks whereon you write shall be in your hand before their eyes" (Ezek. 37:20).

Why all of this attention given to the tiny state of Israel? What is so important about these people? That's a good question.

First of all, the prosperity of the world (yes, I said the world) depends upon the prosperity of Israel. The psalmist said:

> *Let the people praise You, O God; let all the people praise You. O let the nations be glad and sing for joy: for You shall judge the people righteously, and govern the nations upon earth. Selah. Let the people praise You, O God; let all the people praise you. Then shall the earth yield her increase; and God, even our own God, shall bless us. God shall bless us; and all the ends of the earth shall fear Him* (Ps. 67:3-7).

God raised up Israel out of the loins of Abraham and the womb of Sarah. Incidentally, they were idol worshippers when the Lord revealed Himself to them.

From these two would come the nation of Israel. In fact, until Jesus came, Israel was the only nation in the world that was monotheistic, meaning they worshipped one God—Jehovah. Every other country in the world was polytheistic, meaning they worshipped many gods, mainly demon spirits.

Israel had the responsibility of doing three things:

1. Give the world the Word of God, which they did, which was given to them by the means of the prophets and the apostles.

2. Serve as the womb of the Messiah, the Redeemer of humanity, who would ultimately come, one named Jesus.

3. Evangelize the world, which in a sense they did through the apostle Paul.

However, sadly and regrettably, they did not know their Messiah when He actually did come and, thereby, crucified Him and destroyed themselves; however, God has made many promises to the prophets of old, and those promises will be kept.

So, despite the fact of Israel crucifying her Messiah and being scattered all over the world for 2,000 years, the promises of God are that the Lord will bring them back, which He will. They then will accept Christ as Saviour, as Lord, and as their Messiah, which will take place at the second coming. In fact, were it not for the second coming, Israel would be totally destroyed. They will be saved by the very one they crucified. Please understand that when Jesus comes back this second time, He is coming back crowned King of kings and Lord of lords, with a power such as the world has never known before. In fact, the Antichrist will feel the full brunt of that power, with him and his army totally destroyed and Jesus then setting up the kingdom. He (Jesus) will rule that kingdom personally, which will last for a thousand years, and actually forever. In short, that is why these people called Jews or Israelis are so very, very important.

AND BRING THEM INTO THEIR OWN LAND

"And say unto them, Thus says the Lord GOD*; Behold, I will take the children of Israel from among the heathen, whither they be gone,*

and will gather them on every side, and bring them into their own land" (Ezek. 37:21). This verse was chosen for the legend on the Zionist medal commemoration—the First National Federation (1896) since the days of Titus, which was AD 70.

Let us say it again: it is amazing that the Lord would take something as simple as sticks, which Ezekiel literally did, to express and portray something of such vital consequence.

As previously stated, Ezekiel 37:21 began to be fulfilled in 1948. Then, after some 2,000 years of being scattered all over the world and literally ceasing to be a nation, a nation was formed at that time in the exact boundaries given in the Bible. As well, it was named Israel despite the protests from many others. All of this was a move of God unprecedented.

However, the greater fulfillment will be at the second coming when virtually every Jew on the face of the earth will come to Israel and there take up their abode. Then Israel will finally carry out that which the Lord desired of them so long ago. They, in fact, will become the greatest nation on the face of the earth at that time. Then the world will be greatly blessed.

THE LAND

"And I will make them one nation in the land upon the mountains of Israel; and one king shall be king to them all: and they shall be no more two nations, neither shall they be divided into two kingdoms anymore at all" (Ezek. 37:22).

This passage refers to the area promised to Abraham, which Israel never fully realized (Gen. 12:7).

According to that which the Lord gave to Abraham, and which Israel will definitely possess in the coming kingdom age, plus, no doubt, more besides, its boundary on the west is the Mediterranean; on the south, the Suez Canal, which includes the Arabian Peninsula; on the east, the Euphrates River; and on the north, the northern border of Lebanon, plus Syria.

David came closer to occupying the entirety of the Promised Land than anyone else. However, for the greater part of its existence, the territory was much reduced, incorporating basically what was called "from Dan to Beersheba." However, in the coming kingdom age, all of the original promised territory will be occupied, with possibly even extra space added.

Due to this being promised by the Lord to the sons of Jacob, Satan has contested it mightily! Of course, the entirety of the world is aware of the territorial demands made by the Arabs in Israel and their being granted the Gaza Strip plus Jericho, with the entirety of the West Bank possibly to be included.

It is ironic that in July 1994, the newly formed state of Palestine advertised the city of Jerusalem as Jerusalem, Palestine. Israel was highly offended by this action, as it should have been! However, it is well-known that the nations of the world will not recognize Jerusalem as the capital of Israel but, instead, look to Tel Aviv.

Irrespective of the present claims, this land belongs to Israel and is promised so by the Lord. To be sure, this promise will be carried out and fulfilled in totality.

Incidentally, the Arabs in Israel refer to themselves as Palestinians, but the truth is, there is no such people by that name.

The Arabs who occupy part of Israel are Jordanians, Egyptians, Syrians, etc.

SAVED OUT OF IT

"Neither shall they defile themselves any more with their idols, nor with their detestable things, nor with any of their transgressions: but I will save them out of all their dwellingplaces, wherein they have sinned, and will cleanse them: so shall they be My people, and I will be their God" (Ezek. 37:23).

This Scripture will be fulfilled in totality almost immediately after the second coming of Christ, and will bring about that which the Lord has always intended—His people and, consequently, their God.

However, for this to come to pass, it's going to take the great tribulation, which the prophet Jeremiah referred to as *"the time of Jacob's trouble,"* but then he said, *"but he shall be saved out of it"* (Jer. 30:7).

In fact, the great tribulation will be worse on this planet, and especially for Israel, than anything the world has ever seen before. Jesus said so (Mat. 24:21). Sadly, it will take this to bend the stiff neck of the Jewish people, inasmuch as they will then cry to the Lord as they've never cried before because it looks as though it will be the time of their annihilation. What Haman, Herod, and Hitler could not do, it will look as if the Man of Sin, the Antichrist, will carry it out. However, his effort at the annihilation of the Jewish people will be interrupted by the second coming of the Lord, with the Lord coming with such power as the world has never known before. It will be the finish of the Antichrist and his army.

DAVID

"And David My servant shall be king over them; and they all shall have one shepherd: they shall also walk in My judgments, and observe My statutes, and do them" (Ezek. 37:24). The phrase, *"And David My servant shall be king over them,"* is meant to be taken literally. David was ever looked at as the example for all the kings of Israel and will consequently serve in this capacity under Christ forever.

A self-righteous church has difficulty understanding this, especially due to David's transgression regarding Bathsheba and her husband Uriah; however, only self-righteousness would blanch at such a prospect. To those who truly understand who and what man actually is and that the grace of God is our only hope, this passage is a source of great comfort.

Even though David suffered terribly so for this transgression, still, this sin, plus all the other sins that David committed, were washed away by the precious blood of Jesus Christ. It is called justification by faith and it is the undergirding strength of all who trust in the name of Christ.

JUSTIFICATION BY FAITH

The great question is, how can God, who must ever abide by His righteous nature, declare a person who is obviously guilty as "not guilty"?

Paul said, *"To declare, I say, at this time His righteousness: that He might be just, and the justifier of him which believes in Jesus"* (Rom. 3:26).

So, the same question may be asked in this way: How can God be just and, at the same time, be the justifier of the person who is obviously guilty?

The answer is found in the latter portion of Romans 3:26: *"which believes in Jesus."*

Justification is a declaration of not guilty, and to take it even further, it actually means "totally innocent, having never been guilty of any transgression or iniquity."

Now we ask the question again, how can God maintain His justice and, at the same time, justify guilty sinners? Once again, the answer is found in Christ and Christ alone. More particularly, it is found in what Christ did at the cross.

The idea is that Jesus paid the price at Calvary's cross, and faith exhibited in Him by anyone, even the vilest sinner, will actually grant that person a perfect, spotless, imputed righteousness. This is because Jesus has paid it all, and our faith is unequivocally placed in Him.

SUBSTITUTION AND IDENTIFICATION

For this great work of justification to be carried out, God would have to become man, which we refer to as the incarnation. He would have to be man's substitute, doing for man what man could not do for himself. For proper justification to be carried out, Christ would have to be born of a virgin exactly as prophesied by Isaiah (Isa. 7:14). That virgin's name was Mary. Christ's birth had to be in this manner in order that He not have original sin, which came upon all men after the fall. It is referred to as the fallen sons of Adam's lost race. Adam's fall doomed the entirety of the human race except for Christ. In Him and Him alone can we have eternal life.

THE LAST ADAM

As the perfect Son of God, in fact, the last Adam, Jesus had to keep the law perfectly and in every respect. In other words, He could not sin in word, thought, or deed. Had He done so, not only would man be eternally lost with no possible way for anyone to be saved, but likewise, God would be defeated, with Satan becoming the lord of the universe. So, everything was riding on the Lord Jesus Christ. In other words, God placed everything in Jesus Christ, and did so because of His great love for fallen humanity (Jn. 3:16).

Not only did Christ have to live a perfect life, thereby, keeping the law in every respect, but, as well, the terrible sin debt, which included every human being who had ever lived, had piled higher and higher through the centuries.

This debt had to be addressed, had to be paid, and had to be paid in full. For that to happen, which would atone for all sin, Jesus had to go to the cross. He had to give His life because His life was a perfect life, which He gave by the shedding of His blood. Peter referred to it as *"precious blood"* (I Pet. 1:19).

God accepted the sacrifice, meaning that Jesus had taken our place, and now sinful man could be justified.

———⟶—◇—⟵———

Oh! For a faith that will not shrink,
Though pressed by every foe,
That will not tremble on the brink
Of any earthly woe;

That will not murmur or complain
Beneath the chastening rod,
But in the hour of grief or pain
Will lean upon its God;

A faith that shines more bright and clear
When tempests rage without,
That when in danger knows no fear,
In darkness feels no doubt:

That bares unmoved the world's dread frown,
Nor heeds its scornful smile;
That seas of trouble cannot drown,
Or Satan's arts beguile;

A faith that keeps the narrow way
Till life's last hour is fled,
And with a pure and heavenly ray
Illumes a dying bed."

Lord, give us such a faith as this,
And then whatever may come,
We'll taste, even here, the hallowed bliss
Of an eternal home.

CHAPTER 4

FAITH

FAITH

"THEREFORE BEING JUSTIFIED by faith, we have peace with God through our Lord Jesus Christ" (Rom. 5:1).

HOW WAS MAN TO RECEIVE JUSTIFICATION?

So, what does it mean to be justified by faith? In Romans 4 and 5, Paul goes to great length to portray to the human family that justification is not at all obtained by works or merit but strictly by faith. He goes to this great length simply because there is something in man that seeks to earn his way with the Lord. It's a result of the fall, but it is the biggest problem faced by the human family. We keep trying to do for ourselves, which we cannot do. Even if we could do for ourselves, that is, after a measure, God couldn't accept it because of our fallen condition. God can only accept what His Son and our Saviour, the Lord Jesus Christ, has done, and that alone.

WHAT DO WE MEAN BY FAITH?

It means that the believing sinner (and the Christian for that matter) must ever have Christ and the cross as the object of his or her faith. Christ must not be separated from the cross, and, of course, the cross must not be separated from Christ. We aren't meaning that Christ is still on a cross. Actually, He is seated by the right hand of the Father in heaven, but we are rather speaking of what He accomplished at the cross.

To evidence faith in Christ and the cross proclaims the fact that we firmly believe in what He there did for us, and we accept it at face value (Jn. 3:16; Rom. 6:3-5; Eph. 2:13-18; Col. 2:10-15).

So, at the moment the believing sinner evidences faith in Christ and believes what Jesus did for us at the cross, the Lord imputes to that individual a spotless righteousness. In effect, this means that one has been totally and completely justified.

As it concerns justification by faith, Paul said, *"For if by one man's offence* (Adam) *death reigned by one* (as a result of the fall)*; much more they which receive abundance of grace and of the gift of righteousness* (which we receive by accepting Christ and what He did for us at the cross) *shall reign* (rule) *in life by one, Jesus Christ.* (Christ is the source while the cross is the means)*"* (Rom. 5:17).

MY SERVANT DAVID

"And they shall dwell in the land that I have given unto Jacob my servant, wherein your fathers have dwelt; and they shall dwell therein,

even they, and their children, and their children's children forever: and My servant David shall be their prince forever" (Ezek. 37:25).

The phrase of my heading goes back to the messianic promise of II Samuel 7:12-16.

Some have concluded that the name, David, as used here, refers to the Messiah; however, the Holy Spirit uses the phrase, *"My servant David,"* but never once is Christ called "My servant David." So, it is obvious that King David is the one predicted here to be their prince forever under Christ.

There is no evidence that restored Israel will have glorified bodies as all the saints will have in the coming resurrection (I Cor. 15:51-57); however, this refers only to the Israel of that particular time. Every Jew before this time who died in Christ will definitely have glorified bodies.

In fact, the glorified saints will no longer marry and have children because such is not necessary due to our living eternally. Regarding such, Jesus said they *"are as the angels"* (Mat. 22:30).

RESTORED ISRAEL WILL MARRY AND HAVE CHILDREN

Let us say it again: Restored Israel, not having glorified bodies, will continue to marry and have children, even forever. As well, there will be no death, and all will remain youthful and alive by partaking of the fruit and the leaves of the trees beside the river that will flow from the millennial temple in Jerusalem. The Scripture says, *"And the leaf thereof for medicine"* (Ezek. 47:1, 9, 12).

Ezekiel 37:25 mentions *"their children, and their children's children"* forever, proving that babies will continue to be born by these individuals forever.

Therefore, there will be two types of people on the earth forever—the glorified saints of God and those who live in their natural bodies.

The glorified saints will be made up of all included in the first resurrection—both Jews and Gentiles. This will pertain to every person who trusted the Lord for salvation, all the way from Adam through the great tribulation.

The second group will be those who live in their natural bodies forever after having accepted Christ as their eternal Saviour, which will be done after the second coming; consequently, the Bible teaches eternal generations of eternal people on earth. In this second group, there will also be those who will serve God but will not live for Him. They will ultimately die lost (Rev. 20).

THE EVERLASTING COVENANT

"Moreover I will make a covenant of peace with them; it shall be an everlasting covenant with them: and I will place them, and multiply them, and will set My sanctuary in the midst of them for evermore" (Ezek. 37:26). The covenant spoken of in this verse is actually the new covenant (Heb. 13:20). This new covenant has been in force from the time that Jesus Christ died on the cross of Calvary. It was put into force on the day of Pentecost and will actually last forever. It is all based on what Jesus did at the cross, which, in effect, is the very meaning of the

new covenant, i.e., everlasting covenant. This covenant is based on better promises than all the other covenants (Heb. 8:6-13) and, in fact, is a perfect covenant because it is all in Christ, which means it will never have to be amended.

One might say and, thereby, understand it better that Jesus Christ is the new covenant. By that, I don't mean that He knows the new covenant or has the new covenant, but rather He *is* the new covenant. The cross of Christ is the meaning of that covenant, the meaning of which was given to the apostle Paul, and He gave it to us in His 14 epistles.

I WILL BE THEIR GOD,
THEY SHALL BE MY PEOPLE

"My tabernacle also shall be with them: yes, I will be their God, and they shall be My people" (Ezek. 37:27). This verse means that when Jesus Christ comes back in that which is referred to as the second coming, He will come back crowned King of kings and Lord of lords.

As well, He is going to be the president, so to speak, of the entirety of the world. In other words, every single leader of every nation in the world will answer to Him and to Him alone. In fact, the Scripture says that *"the government shall be upon His shoulder: and His name shall be called Wonderful, Counsellor, The mighty God, the everlasting Father, The Prince of Peace"* (Isa. 9:6).

Then it says, *"Of the increase of His government and peace there shall be no end, upon the throne of David, and upon His kingdom, to order it, and to establish it with judgment and with justice from henceforth even forever. The zeal of the* LORD *of Hosts will perform this"* (Isa. 9:7).

Actually, the first part of this verse has reference to the fact that there will not be an immediate subjugation of the earth upon the Lord's return, but the Messiah's kingdom shall ever increase more and more until it ultimately fills the entirety of the earth.

MY SANCTUARY

"And the heathen shall know that I the LORD *do sanctify Israel, when My sanctuary shall be in the midst of them for evermore"* (Ezek. 37:28).

In the coming kingdom age, when the Lord will reign over the earth for a thousand years, and then forever, Israel will finally come to the place that the Lord intended all along. In other words, she will accept her Saviour and Messiah, the Lord Jesus Christ, and then will be promoted by the Lord to be the leading nation in the world.

God's presence with Israel is the sign that He is with them and that the world must and, in fact, shall recognize this approval.

The sanctuary in the midst of Israel is the greatest sign of all of God's acceptance and approval. In fact, the last nine chapters of the book of Ezekiel proclaim what this sanctuary will be like. Actually, the very last phrase in the book of Ezekiel is, *"The* LORD *is there"* (Ezek. 48:35). There could be nothing greater than that!

THE WORD OF THE LORD

"And the word of the LORD *came unto me, saying"* (Ezek. 38:1).

Ezekiel 36 portrays the restoration of Israel, while Chapters 37 and 38 proclaim how this restoration is to take place. It will be by the Spirit of God.

Immediately after the coming of the Holy Spirit (Ezek. 37:14), Satan rears his ugly head. Ezekiel 38 portrays the highest ascendancy of man in the form of the Antichrist. He will be empowered by Satan as no man has ever been empowered by the Evil One, and he will attempt to usurp authority over the Holy Spirit and to destroy the ancient people—God's people. It is called the battle of Armageddon.

THE SPIRIT COMES, AND SATAN OPPOSES

The chronological order of these chapters, at least in the spiritual sense, is the pattern always followed by Satan: the Holy Spirit comes, and Satan opposes. In fact, Satan has no regard at all for the efforts of man, be they ever so religious. His opposition is stirred only upon the advent of the Holy Spirit as given by Christ; consequently, the far greater majority of the world of religion, even including the church, experiences no opposition from Satan whatsoever. Actually, he is the author of all religion and much of that which goes under the guise of Christianity.

Nevertheless, for the few (and few it is) who operate in the realm of the Holy Spirit and the Word of God and depend upon the empowerment, leading, and anointing, the opposition by the

Evil One is fierce indeed. No opposition, no Holy Spirit; much opposition, much Holy Spirit. Actually, even as we will study, these two chapters—Ezekiel 38 and 39— constitute the greatest detailed account in the Bible of the battle of Armageddon.

GOG

"*Son of man, set your face against Gog, the land of Magog, the chief prince of Meshech and Tubal, and prophesy against him*" (Ezek. 38:2). This verse proclaims the very opposite of what the prophet now was commanded to do as it regarded prophesying blessing upon Israel (Ezek. 37:4), which portrayed God's favor. The prophet was now commanded to do the very opposite against the confederation of Satan. He would prophesy against him.

As the favorable prophecy concerning the restoration of Israel is dead certain to be fulfilled, likewise, the unfavorable prophecy against the Antichrist, Satan's chief henchman, will most assuredly come to pass.

The name or title "Gog" means "roof or mountain." Likewise, this is the name of the giant Ishbibenob, who tried to kill David at the close of his reign. It means "dweller on the mount," signifying the efforts of man regarding ascendancy in pomp, pride, and power, with Gog being the ultimate.

NAMES OF THE ANTICHRIST

Among the several names that will be used regarding the Antichrist, Gog is definitely one of those names. The Holy Spirit ascribing this name to him in no way means that it is guaranteed that the Antichrist will employ the same. While he may definitely use the name, the main purpose of the Spirit is to portray the fact that the spirit of the Antichrist is saying that the mountain, i.e., the entirety of the earth, is his.

In fact, the Antichrist will go under several names:

- The *"little horn"* (Dan. 7 and 8).
- The *"prince who shall come"* (Dan. 9).
- The *"king of the north"* (Dan. 11).
- The *"man of sin"* (II Thess. 2).
- The *"son of perdition"* (II Thess. 2).
- *"That Wicked"* (II Thess. 2).
- The *"king of Babylon"* (Isa. 13 and 14)
- *"The Assyrian"* (Mic. 5).
- The *"Antichrist"* (I Jn. 2).
- *"The beast"* (Rev. 13).

All of these Scriptures speak of a man who will come in the last days, which compares with Ezekiel 38 and 39.

GENTILES

The phrase of Ezekiel 38:2, *"The land of Magog, the chief prince of Meshech and Tubal,"* merely refers to the Gentiles who descended from Japheth. Magog, Meshech, and Tubal were sons of Japheth, who was a son of Noah (Gen. 10:1–4).

Some have tried to make the land of Magog refer to Russia; however, it simply refers to the area populated by the sons of Japheth, who populated Eastern and Western Europe.

To fully understand these phrases, one has to go back to the time of Noah and make a brief study of his three sons—Shem, Ham, and Japheth. From these three sons came the entirety of the human family.

As stated, Japheth's descendants settled Europe, which ultimately settled North America, as well as parts of the East. They are known as the Gentiles.

Shem produced those who settled the Middle East, as well as Asia Minor.

Ham's descendants, as well, settled parts of the Middle East, Africa, and ultimately Central and South America (Gen. 10).

As is obvious, the descendants of Japheth and Ham make up the greater majority of the greater population of the world, with the sons of Shem basically referring to the Israelites and the Arabs.

Noah actually prophesied what would happen to the descendants of his three sons.

SHEM

The Holy Spirit through Noah said, *"Blessed be the LORD God of Shem"* (Gen. 9:26), meaning that the relationship between the Lord and the descendants of Shem would be closer than any other. In fact, through Shem would come the Bible, the Word of God, and most important of all, Christ would be after this lineage (Gen. 10:21; 11:10; Lk. 3:23–38).

Through the family of Shem would come the Israelites and the Arabs, both in the line of Abraham. The two sons of Abraham,

Isaac and Ishmael, would bring forth the entire lineage of Shem. The Israelites, God's chosen, would come from Isaac, while the Arabs would come from Ishmael. The Lord rejected Ishmael as a work of the flesh even though He blessed him (Gen. 17:20). However, the Lord said that He would bless and establish His covenant with Isaac (Gen. 17:19); consequently, there has been great contention between Isaac and Ishmael ever since!

The true seed, the Lord Jesus Christ, God manifest in the flesh, came through the lineage of Isaac, while the false seed, Muhammad, came through Ishmael.

The work of the Holy Spirit as produced through Abraham (the Lord Jesus Christ) has blessed the entirety of the world. However, the work of the flesh as produced also by Abraham, which resulted in the birth of Ishmael, has brought great contention to the world, as do all works of the flesh (Gen. 17:19–22).

HAM

The Scripture says that the youngest son of Noah *"saw the nakedness of his father"* (Gen. 9:22), which some Bible scholars think may have included the homosexual act. This included Ham's son, Canaan, and resulted in the Holy Spirit through Noah saying, *"Cursed be Canaan"* (Gen. 9:25). Consequently, Ham's descendants through Canaan have been cursed exactly as prophesied.

The descendants of Canaan settled in the Middle East, making up the Jebusites, Hivites, Philistines, etc., and were ultimately destroyed by Israel, or else, made servants upon the taking of the Promised Land. They also populated Africa.

Therefore, as already stated, the land of Magog, although including Russia, also includes Europe, the Far East, North America, etc.

JAPHETH

The Holy Spirit through Noah said of Japheth, *"God shall enlarge Japheth"* (Gen. 9:27).

This prophecy has come true to the letter in that the races that sprang from Japheth, the white and the yellow, have been the driving force all over the world as it pertains to science, government, etc.

The remaining statement concerning Japheth, *"And he shall dwell in the tents of Shem"* (Gen. 9:27), refers to Israel originally destined by God to be the leading people in the world, but they forfeited this position because of sin; therefore, that which was promised to Shem (leader of the world) was instead given by God to Japheth, i.e., his descendants.

This has reference to Israel losing her way with God and the scepter of power being transferred from the kings of Judah to the Gentiles, of which the first was Nebuchadnezzar. The last king of Judah was Zedekiah, and the last king in the Davidic line to grace the throne of Judah, which was the last king actually recognized by God, was the king who immediately preceded Zedekiah, Jehoiachin. The power has remained with the Gentiles ever since, with Christ calling it *"the times of the Gentiles"* (Lk. 21:24).

This is what is meant by Japheth dwelling *"in the tents of Shem"* (Gen. 9:27).

THE CHIEF PRINCE OF MESHECH AND TUBAL

"And say, Thus says the Lord GOD; Behold, I am against you, O Gog, the chief prince of Meshech and Tubal" (Ezek. 38:3). This verse proclaims the Holy Spirit some 2,500 years ago speaking through the prophet Ezekiel and portraying the disposition of the Lord as it regards the coming Antichrist.

For many years Bible teachers taught that these passages refer to Russia, but a closer investigation of the statements proves otherwise. As well, the events that have transpired recently in the area formerly known as the Soviet Union further emphasize the fact that even though Russia will, no doubt, play a part in these last-day events, still, it will only be a part of the whole.

Therefore, the phrase, *"Behold, I am against you, O Gog,"* is not really referring to Russia but, instead, the Antichrist.

For years Bible scholars have erroneously attempted to make the name *Meshech* mean Moscow, and *Tubal* mean Tobolsk, both in Russia; however, these two names, Meshech and Tubal, have no reference to the cities mentioned but, instead, refer to the whole of Europe. As well, as Daniel portrays, this fits in perfectly with his prophecies. Actually, when the Antichrist makes his debut in the battle of Armageddon, his vast army will include myriads of soldiers from both Europe and the Far East.

THE BATTLE OF ARMAGEDDON

"And I will turn you back, and put hooks into your jaws, and I will bring you forth, and all your army, horses and horsemen, all of

them clothed with all sorts of armor, even a great company with bucklers and shields, all of them handling swords" (Ezek. 38:4). This verse refers to the battle of Armageddon, which will be the second invasion of Israel by the Antichrist, in which he will be totally destroyed.

Approximately seven years before, the Antichrist will have signed a seven-year peace treaty with Israel and other nations. In fact, all of these accords that we are presently seeing between Israel and the so-called Palestinians, etc., are merely precursors of the seven-year treaty that will be formulated by the Antichrist. At the moment the Antichrist signs that seven-year treaty, the great tribulation will begin.

At that time Israel, thinking the Antichrist is the Messiah and announcing such to the entirety of the world, will say, "Peace and safety." However, then Paul said, "Sudden destruction comes upon them, as travail upon a woman with child; and they shall not escape" (I Thess. 5:3).

At the midpoint of this seven-year treaty (Dan. 9:27; 11:40–45; II Thess. 2:3–4; Rev. 11:1–2), the Antichrist will break his treaty with Israel and attack her, with Israel suffering her first military defeat since her formation as a nation in 1948. Now will truly begin the "time of Jacob's trouble" (Jer. 30:7). For those three and one-half years, it will look as though the Antichrist will be able to do what Haman, Herod, and Hitler failed to do.

Actually, he would succeed but for the second coming of the Lord Jesus Christ with the armies of heaven, who will defeat him in what is called the battle of Armageddon. The Lord will then set up His kingdom of righteousness (Zech. 14:1–15; Rev. 19:11–21).

WEAPONS OF WAR

If one is to notice, words such as *horses, bucklers,* and *shields,* as well as *swords,* are used because this was the weaponry of that day; however, the weapons that will be used by the Antichrist will be modern weaponry with the newest technology.

No, there is no scriptural evidence that the Antichrist will use atomic bombs, etc. Quite possibly he will not do so simply because Israel is equipped with atomic weapons as well. Wherein the use of such may well destroy Israel, still, the Antichrist would be destroyed also.

The Holy Spirit used the words He did regarding weapons because they are familiar to all and properly explain what needs to be explained. In fact, if modern terminology had been used, such as jets, bombers, machine guns, etc., these words would have had no meaning until the recent past; therefore, such would have caused endless controversy among Bible scholars. The idea is not to name the weaponry, but rather to show that the Antichrist will be fully equipped with all sorts of weapons, determined to destroy Israel.

THE TAUNT

"Persia, Ethiopia, and Libya with them; all of them with shield and helmet: Gomer, and all his bands; the house of Togarmah of

the north quarters, and all his bands: and many people with you" (Ezek. 38:5-6). These verses proclaim the names of some of the nations that will throw in their lot with the Antichrist, determined to help him take over the entirety of the world.

The countries here named only include a few of the total that will join in with the Antichrist. Actually, these countries, plus scores not named, will throw in their lot with the Man of Sin. At the beginning of the kingdom age when our Lord will stand as the leader of the entirety of the world, the judgment of the nations will take place. Then, scores of these nations will literally cease to be.

Concerning this, the words of our Lord are: *"When the Son of Man shall come in His glory, and all the holy angels with Him, then shall He sit upon the throne of His glory: and before Him shall be gathered all nations: and He shall separate them one from another, as a shepherd divides his sheep from the goats: and He shall set the sheep on His right hand, but the goats on the left"* (Mat. 25:31-33).

The sheep nations, so to speak, will be those that tried to help Israel, or at least did not join in with the Antichrist.

The goat nations are those who will have fought against Israel and will literally cease to be (Mat. 25:40-46). As stated, this will take place at the beginning of the kingdom age.

THE ANSWER GIVEN BY THE HOLY SPIRIT

"Be you prepared, and prepare for yourself, you, and all your company who are assembled unto you, and be you a guard unto them" (Ezek. 38:7).

As the Antichrist will give his taunt, claiming that he will destroy Israel, likewise, the Holy Spirit will give His taunt, throwing the words of the man of sin back into his face. In essence, Ezekiel 38:7 literally proclaims the taunt as given by the Holy Spirit to the Antichrist.

In other words, He will say, "Prepare yourself to the very best of your ability, and, still, it will avail you nothing as you will be totally defeated."

The phrase, *"And be you a guard unto them,"* refers to this mighty army under the leadership of the Antichrist thinking that, due to their past successes, his leadership will guarantee continued successes.

However, the balance of this chapter will tell exactly what will happen to all those *"who are assembled unto you."*

THE LATTER YEARS

"After many days you shall be visited: in the latter years you shall come into the land that is brought back from the sword, and is gathered out of many people, against the mountains of Israel, which have been always waste: but it is brought forth out of the nations, and they shall dwell safely all of them" (Ezek. 38:8). Two phrases in this verse, *"After many days"* and *"in the latter years,"* refer to this present time and the immediate future; therefore, any claims that this chapter has already been fulfilled are spurious.

The Holy Spirit, no doubt, gave these phrases through Ezekiel in order to dispel the idea among the exiles that this particular prophecy pertained to their times. This that is being said is to be fulfilled in the latter years, which, as stated, refers to this present time and the near future.

The phrase, *"The land that is brought back from the sword,"* refers to the many conflicts Israel has had since becoming a nation in 1948. Even though the United Nations voted that the Jews be given their ancient homeland, still, it was definitely not a peaceful transition. The Muslims repeatedly tried to stop her and due to their great numbers, would have definitely succeeded had it not been for the help of the Lord. So, Israel was literally brought back from the sword.

GATHERED

The phrase in Ezekiel 38:8, *"And is gathered out of many people,"* refers to Jews that were scattered all over the world but began to come to the newly formed state of Israel, beginning in 1948. In fact, Jews are still coming from many nations of the world to Israel, with the last great influx being from the former Soviet Union.

The phrase, *"Against the mountains of Israel, which have been always waste,"* refers to the land of Palestine that virtually went to waste after AD 70 when Titus, the Roman general, totally destroyed Jerusalem, slaughtering over 1 million Jews and selling hundreds of thousands of others as slaves.

Coupled with the second onslaught by the Romans in AD 150, the Jews were driven all over the world, with their ancient homeland reverting basically to waste.

The phrase, *"But it is brought forth out of the nations,"* refers to the United Nations voting that Israel would become a state, with even Soviet Russia voting her approval.

DWELL SAFELY

The last phrase in Ezekiel 38:8, *"And they shall dwell safely all of them,"* refers to the Jews desiring a homeland instead of being scattered all over the world. Their feeling was that if this could be obtained, then they would be safe.

The Holocaust of World War II, which saw some 6 million Jews slaughtered by Hitler, caused the birth of a desire in the hearts of many, many Jews to insist upon this homeland. While that desire had been there for many years, now it took on a new incentive.

During the tumultuous days of 1948 when the Jews were struggling to gain the approval of the United Nations (especially the United States) to secure a homeland, one Jew was asked exactly why they wanted such. His answer was somewhat enlightening. With a far-away look in his eyes, and his mind, no doubt, reliving the horror of the recent Holocaust, he said, "The next time they'll know where to find us, and we will be ready."

After nearly 2,000 years, Jacob was finally coming home.

As I dictate these notes, I strongly sense the presence of God in that we are so privileged to be living during the time when these great prophecies of old are beginning to be fulfilled. What a testimony to the veracity of the Word of God! What a testimony to the truthfulness of its eternal composition! But yet, even though they have in part dwelled safely, still, the safety of Israel, even from its beginning, has been precarious.

In the very near future, Israel, continuing to be pressed from all sides, will eagerly accept the promises of the false messiah—the Antichrist—thinking he fulfills the prophecies and will guarantee the safety for which they have so long sought, but it will prove to be a false hope.

However, upon the second coming of Christ, then and truly, *"They shall dwell safely all of them."*

ARMAGEDDON

"You shall ascend and come like a storm, you shall be like a cloud to cover the land, you, and all your bands, and many people with you" (Ezek. 38:9). The phrase in this verse, *"You shall ascend and come like a storm,"* proclaims the battle of Armageddon. It will be the most horrifying conflict the world has ever known, at least concerning one particular battle. Hundreds of thousands, and possibly even millions, will die.

The phrase, *"You shall be like a cloud to cover the land,"* refers to tremendous numbers of soldiers of the Antichrist. This will result in many deaths, especially considering that we are speaking of the Lord intervening and Zechariah saying that He will *"fight against those nations, as when He fought in the day of battle"* (Zech. 14:3).

At any rate, the battle will be so severe and the deaths of such magnitude that it is said that the blood (winepress) will flow to *"the horse bridles, by the space of a thousand and six hundred furlongs,"* referring to about 184 miles (Rev. 14:20).

This will, no doubt, be blood mixed with water because Ezekiel will mention an overflowing rain (Ezek. 38:22).

So, we are speaking here of something that has never happened in such magnitude as this in the history of the world.

AN EVIL THOUGHT

"Thus says the Lord GOD; It shall also come to pass, that at the same time shall things come into your mind, and you shall think an evil thought" (Ezek. 38:10).

The evil thought of the Antichrist constitutes the destruction of Israel. Unfortunately, untold numbers have harbored the same type of thought over the many past centuries, and do so presently.

However, let it be known that all who harbor evil thoughts against Israel are at the same time harboring evil thoughts against God. To say the least, such is a losing operation!

To be sure, the Man of Sin will have plans inspired of Satan to destroy Israel and the Jews. He thinks that he will do what Haman, Herod, and Hitler could not do! In his hatred of God, and especially the Lord Jesus Christ, and due to the fact that the church has been raptured away, the Antichrist will center the focus of his anger and evil on the Jews. They, by and large, will be the only organized people connected to the Lord on the face of the earth. So, at least in his mind, upon their destruction, he will be master and god of the world (II Thess. 2:4).

The worth of the land of Israel is not actually that important. In fact, it makes up only one-sixth of 1 percent of the land of the Middle East presently held by the Arabs. So, why is this so all-important to the Antichrist?

THE PROBLEM IS SPIRITUAL

The problem is spiritual, even as it has always been spiritual. God called Abraham out of Ur of the Chaldees after having revealed Himself to the Patriarch, which would be followed by tremendous promises.

In fact, from the loins of Abraham and the womb of Sarah, his wife, would come the people of faith, who were destined by God to give the world the Word of God and to bring forth the Messiah.

Accordingly, they would govern the world; however, they rejected their Messiah and crucified Him, which means that they refused the kingdom that was offered to them.

As a result of this and because of the chastising hand of God, their nation was destroyed, and they were scattered all over the world. But yet, the promises remained, and they most definitely will be fulfilled.

Knowing all of this, at least what the Lord has predicted concerning these ancient people, Satan, even from the beginning, has set out to stop the fulfillment of the promises of God respecting Israel and her restoration. In other words, the opposition has been relentless. Satan knows that if Israel falls, the promises of God also fall.

CANNOT SATAN READ THE BIBLE?

The idea is that Satan can certainly read the Bible and can certainly understand what it says. It predicts his total and complete defeat. So, how does he think that he can overcome the Lord?

The truth is, Satan is deceived, even as the billions who follow him. He actually believes that he will win in this conflict. It is the most profound case of unbelief in the history of man, which has dragged down untold millions, even billions, into eternal darkness.

However, the truth is that he will not succeed. Every single promise and prediction in the Bible that has not already been fulfilled will be fulfilled to the letter. Of that, one can be certain.

THE ATTACK ON ISRAEL

"And you shall say, I will go up to the land of unwalled villages; I will go to them who are at rest, who dwell safely, all of them dwelling without walls, and having neither bars nor gates" (Ezek. 38:11). This verse presents the Antichrist now engaging the final solution, the total destruction of Israel, with every Jew being killed, or so he thinks.

After the Antichrist breaks his seven-year pact with Israel and actually invades them, making Jerusalem his city and the temple his headquarters, Daniel says that he will hear *"tidings out of the east and out of the north"* (Dan. 11:44), and will have to leave off his subjugation of Israel in order to attend to this pressing business.

Actually, these battles that he will fight at this time will probably take the better part of two years to finish. He will then regroup with even a larger army, having won these conflicts, and will come down to once and for all annihilate Israel.

Incidentally, there is every evidence that at this time America, plus all the other nations in the world, will remain neutral, even though some of them may have previously thought favorably toward Israel (Zech. 12:1–3).

After having been defeated upon the first invasion of the Antichrist, Israel will have fled to Petra in modern Jordan and other places. Upon the Antichrist (Gog) going to fight other battles, Israel will then filter back into the land and reoccupy its cities. She will attempt to make herself strong.

In Ezek. 38:11, the phrases, *"The land of unwalled villages,"* *"dwelling without walls,"* and *"having neither bars nor gates,"* refer to Israel's efforts at mobilization to be rather weak, at least in the mind of the Antichrist. In other words, the Antichrist feels that he will have no problem whatsoever in totally annihilating these people; however, he will reckon without the coming of the Lord.

TO TAKE A SPOIL

"To take a spoil, and to take a prey; to turn your hand upon the desolate places that are now inhabited, and upon the people who are gathered out of the nations, which have gotten cattle and goods, who dwell in the midst of the land" (Ezek. 38:12). This verse presents the plans of the Man of Sin. The Antichrist, at least

at this time, will be well on his way to taking over the entirety of the world.

By comparing Scripture with Scripture, it seems that by now he will have already conquered many nations of the world and neutralized most of the others, if not all, by making agreements with them, etc. His ambition is to rule the world. Power will be given to him by Satan as it has never been given to any other man. Due to this and due to his False Prophet performing miracles, the nations of the world, at least at the outset, will truly think that this man holds the answers to the ills and problems of mankind. These nations will, no doubt, include America as well. This will be man's grandest effort to restore Paradise without the Tree of Life, which is Jesus Christ.

However, according to Revelation 6, his conquest by peace will quickly turn into a conquest by war. By now, his strength is so great that it seems nothing can stand in his way. He will set out to take over the entirety of the world, or so he thinks.

This will be the conclusion of man's social system and man's government. It will be the conclusion of a society that has been corrupt from its very beginning. Now, the corruption will be on a scale heretofore unknown in the history of man. Actually, the world is already being set for the advent of the Antichrist. His rise will be religious as well as political. As such, the apostate church is being jockeyed into position to herald his rise in a positive way.

Let us love, and sing, and wonder,
Let us praise the Saviour's name!
He has hushed the law's loud thunder,
He has quenched Mount Sinai's flame;
He has washed us with His blood,
He has brought us nigh to God.

Let us love the Lord who bought us,
Pitied us when enemies hit us,
Called us by His grace, and taught us,
Gave us ears and gave us eyes:
He has washed us with His blood,
He presents our souls to God.

Let us sing, though fierce temptation
Threaten hard to bear us down!
For the Lord, our strong salvation,
Holds in view the conqueror's crown,
He who washed us with His blood,
Soon will bring us home to God.

Let us wonder; grace and justice
Join and point to mercy's store;
When through grace in Christ our trust is,
Justice smiles and asks no more:
He who washed us with His blood,
Has secured our way to God.

Let us praise and join the chorus
Of the saints enthroned on high;
Here they trusted Him before us
Now their praises fill the sky:
Thou hast washed us with Thy blood;
Thou art worthy, Lamb of God!

.

CHAPTER 5

THE FURY OF GOD

THE FURY OF GOD

"SHEBA, AND DEDAN, and the merchants of Tarshish, with all the young lions thereof, shall say unto you, Are you come to take a spoil? have you gathered your company to take a prey? to carry away silver and gold, to take away cattle and goods, to take a great spoil?" (Ezek. 38:13).

THE QUESTION

Some erroneously teach from this verse that these nations represent opposition to the Antichrist and will, therefore, throw in their lot with Israel, helping to defend her; however, there is nothing in this verse or any other verse in the Bible that says this.

Actually, as we have previously stated, every evidence is that no nation in the world will come to Israel's aid at that time. The great prophet Zechariah said: *"For I will gather all nations against Jerusalem to battle; and the city shall be taken, and the houses rifled, and the women ravished; and half of the city shall go forth into captivity, and the residue of the people shall not be cut off from the city"* (Zech. 14:2).

There is evidence here that every nation in the world will be on the side of the Antichrist. If not directly joining him, they will seek to remain neutral.

There is no evidence that Israel will have any help at all from any other countries in the world.

No doubt, there will be opposition to the Antichrist in many nations of the world; however, such will be muted and will offer no viable protest at this incursion.

DWELL SAFELY

"Therefore, son of man, prophesy and say unto Gog, Thus says the Lord GOD; In that day when My people of Israel dwell safely, shall you not know it?" (Ezek. 38:14).

The idea of this verse is that despite the Antichrist invading Israel and defeating her at the midpoint of the great tribulation and breaking his seven-year pact, still, due to pressing business elsewhere (Dan. 11:44), Israel will filter back into the land. She will reoccupy it and seemingly will once again dwell there with a modicum of safety for a short period of time. The Antichrist will be fighting great battles elsewhere. During that time, which will probably be nearly three years, he will be little threat to Israel.

However, Israel filtering back into the land and dwelling safely will, no doubt, infuriate the Man of Sin, and he will set about to handle the situation once and for all, which will be the battle of Armageddon.

THE NORTH

"And you shall come from your place out of the north parts, you, and many people with you, all of them riding upon horses, a great company, and a mighty army" (Ezek. 38:15). This verse does not refer to Russia as some think, but rather to Syria. This will be where he will gather his army.

However, the Syria of Daniel's prophecies, of which this speaks, includes modern Syria, Lebanon, Iraq, and Iran.

Daniel's prophecies speak of the breakup of the Grecian Empire under Alexander the Great. It broke into four parts, of which the Syrian division, or northern part, signifies the area from which the Antichrist will come (Dan. 11). Therefore, he could come from any one of the several countries mentioned above and still fulfill Bible prophecy.

At the beginning of the time of the Antichrist, 10 kingdoms will be formed inside the old Roman Empire territory. As the Antichrist begins his quest for the world, he will declare war on three of these kingdoms and quickly overcome them (Dan. 7:8-9, 21-25). The other six will throw in their lot with him without conflict, with him now heading up all 10 kingdoms (Rev. 17:9-17).

After attacking Israel and defeating her at about the midpoint of the great tribulation, in fact, breaking his pact with her, this is when the *"tidings out of the east and out of the north"* will come to him (Dan. 11:44). He will then stop his efforts concerning Israel and go north and east to fight great battles. This will, no doubt, bring Russia, and possibly China and Japan, under his wing. He will then come down upon Israel, which is described as the battle of Armageddon (Zech. 14:1–5; Rev. 19:11–21).

THE LATTER DAYS

"And you shall come up against My people of Israel, as a cloud to cover the land; it shall be in the latter days, and I will bring you against My land, that the heathen may know Me, when I shall be sanctified in you, O Gog, before their eyes" (Ezek. 38:16). This verse refers to the last of the last days, which actually pertains to the present and the near future. In other words, these prophecies have already begun to come to pass and will accelerate their fulfillment with each passing day.

The phrase, *"when I shall be sanctified in you, O Gog, before their eyes,"* refers to the Lord defending what is His.

The idea is that Gog will make his boasts all over the world concerning the greatness of his power and the absence of the power of God. No doubt, he will use all of the media to accomplish this task. In other words, every television network in the world will proclaim his intentions.

However, when the Lord does what He has promised to do, all the *"heathen"* will *"know Me."* Then, He will show the world His great power, which will be made evident at the second coming.

THE PROPHETS OF ISRAEL

"Thus says the Lord GOD*; Are you he of whom I have spoken in old time by My servants the prophets of Israel, which prophesied in those days many years that I would bring you against them?"* (Ezek. 38:17). This verse proclaims the fact that the prophets of Israel were the only ones in the world recognized at that time by God.

The Lord is actually speaking here of the prophecies given to Ezekiel, of which this is one, as well as Isaiah and Daniel, along with Zechariah and, no doubt, others.

The phrase, *"old time,"* is in contrast to the *"latter days"* of Ezekiel 38:16.

As well, the Holy Spirit emphasizes the veracity of these prophecies of old time, guaranteeing the certitude of their fulfillment. Actually, the Bible is the only book in the world that prophetically tells the future of man. This alone is enough to prove its veracity and predictions.

Especially considering that approximately one-third of the Bible is made up of prophecy, with great portions of it yet unfulfilled, to doubt the inspiration of such is to doubt the truth that is before one's very eyes. As well, every single prophecy has come to pass according to the fullness of its time, which guarantees the fulfillment of those that are to follow.

Of course, the question must be asked as to the Antichrist reading these very prophecies and then making his plans to circumvent their predictions. That will not be done because of the heart of unbelief in man. The Antichrist will be so lifted up in himself that he will surely think that nothing can stand in his way, and he will, no doubt, make himself believe that all these things, despite their accuracy and pinpoint predictions, are mere myths. Actually, almost the entirety of the world does the same thing presently and, in fact, always has!

FURY

"And it shall come to pass at the same time when Gog shall come against the land of Israel, says the Lord GOD, that My fury shall come up in My face" (Ezek. 38:18).

The phrase, *"that My fury shall come up in My face,"* refers to the actual attack by the Antichrist on the land of Israel. This is the battle of Armageddon (Rev. 14:14-20; 16:16).

In fact, the phrase, *"My fury shall come up in My face,"* corresponds to the statement of Zechariah, *"Then shall the LORD go forth, and fight against those nations, as when He fought in the day of battle"* (Zech. 14:3).

This is anger at a white-hot pitch, and anger from one who is all-powerful; therefore, the world is going to see a magnitude of judgment that it has never known before. The Man of Sin will rue the day that he took on God's people and God's land.

JEALOUSY

"For in My jealousy and in the fire of My wrath have I spoken, Surely in that day there shall be a great shaking in the land of Israel" (Ezek. 38:19). This verse proclaims the fact that God's jealousy is

linked to His fury and wrath. These are His people and His land. He is jealous over them, as He is jealous over all that belongs to Him, including the church, and we speak of the true church.

The phrase, *"Surely in that day there shall be a great shaking in the land of Israel,"* can refer only to the battle of Armageddon, for no other prediction can match this description.

THE PRESENCE OF GOD

"So that the fishes of the sea, and the fowls of the heaven, and the beasts of the field, and all creeping things that creep upon the earth, and all the men who are upon the face of the earth, shall shake at My presence, and the mountains shall be thrown down, and the steep places shall fall, and every wall shall fall to the ground" (Ezek. 38:20). This verse proclaims a display of power such as the world has never known before. As stated, it will take place at the second coming.

This tremendous conflict, and we continue to speak of the second coming, will affect plant life, animal life, plus all humans, and even the topography of the land. All of this will in no way be caused by the Antichrist but, instead, by the power of God. Thusly, one can understand the magnitude of *"My fury* (that) *shall come up in My face."*

Actually, the world has never seen, heard, or known of such power being expended in such magnitude. No wonder the Lord said, *"the heathen may know Me."* He was referring to much of the world who will see this spectacle. It will more than likely be shown over television even as it transpires and will be brought into their very homes.

Undoubtedly, there will be hundreds, if not thousands, of television cameras there. They will be sponsored by the major networks of the world and insisted on by the Antichrist in his pomp and pride. He will desire to record for the entirety of the world the tremendous victory he is about to win, or so he thinks. There will be a victory, but it will not be his!

THE MAGNITUDE OF HIS POWER

The tremendous television coverage, which will be meant to impress the entirety of the world, will do just that, but in the opposite direction. The world will see a demonstration of the power of God as it has never seen before. As well, it will undoubtedly observe Christ with the armies of heaven coming back to earth with a glory that boggles the mind.

This will be quite an event to say the least, especially considering that every born-again individual who has ever lived will be with Christ at His second coming (Jude 1:14). This number will include those who are now reading these very words who are saved by the blood of Christ. Actually, outside of these Scriptures, there is no way for one to describe the magnitude of this power because it is a power far beyond the capabilities of man to even comprehend or understand.

It may be argued that atomic energy falls into the same category; however, as powerful as that is, it is localized, whereas this will cover the entirety of the land of Israel, plus other areas as well.

Some may argue that all of the disturbance in the heavens that will take place at the second coming, which Jesus addressed in Matthew 24, will knock out all television reception. While that certainly could be, there is every evidence that the Lord will protect the television coverage, for the Scripture says concerning the second coming, in the words of our Lord: *"And then shall appear the sign of the Son of man in heaven: and then shall all the tribes of the earth mourn, and they shall see the Son of Man coming in the clouds of heaven with power and great glory"* (Mat. 24:30).

About the only way that all the people of the earth will be able to see Him is by television. Incidentally, that doesn't mean every single person, but rather the greater bulk of the population.

STRANGE HAPPENINGS

"And I will call for a sword against him throughout all My mountains, says the Lord GOD: every man's sword shall be against his brother" (Ezek. 38:21). This verse proclaims one of the methods of destruction employed by the Lord in battles of the past. He has caused the enemy to begin to fight among themselves.

For instance, when Jonathan was fighting the Philistines, the Scripture says, *"The earth quaked"* and *"They went on beating down one another,"* meaning that the Philistines, for some reason, turned on each other (I Sam. 14:15–16). This will happen, as well, at the battle of Armageddon.

HAILSTONES, FIRE, AND BRIMSTONE

"And I will plead against him with pestilence and with blood; and I will rain upon him, and upon his bands, and upon the many

people who are with him, an overflowing rain, and great hailstones, fire, and brimstone" (Ezek. 38:22).

The phrase, *"And I will plead against him with pestilence and with blood,"* refers to different types of destructive forces, which, in this case, will cause great bloodshed.

In fact, the blood shed by the forces of the Antichrist will be so great in the battle of Armageddon that the Scripture says it will flow to the horses' bridles, at least for a certain distance, and will, no doubt, be mixed with the overflowing rain of this verse (Rev. 14:20).

At the battle of Armageddon, the Lord will utilize the elements, with, no doubt, millions of hailstones. Many of these stones will be the size of an automobile coming down upon the army of the Antichrist. Along with such terrible destructive force, it will be accompanied by fire and brimstone. This will be artillery such as the world has never known before. One can imagine what this will do to an army of millions of men packed closely together.

For instance, when the Canaanite general Sisera was defeated by Deborah and Barak, the Scripture says concerning his 900 chariots of iron, *"The earth trembled, and the heavens dropped, the clouds also dropped water."* (Judg. 5:4).

It also said, *"The stars in their courses fought against Sisera"* (Judg. 5:20).

Therefore, the Lord will employ the same tactics in the battle of Armageddon but on a magnified scale. He will use the elements, over which neither the Antichrist nor any other man will have any control.

THE LORD WILL MAGNIFY
AND SANCTIFY HIMSELF

"Thus will I magnify Myself, and sanctify Myself; and I will be known in the eyes of many nations, and they shall know that I am the LORD" (Ezek. 38:23).

The Antichrist has boasted to the world what he is going to do to Israel, and the Lord will now proclaim what He is going to do to the Antichrist. Then shall the entirety of the world know and understand without a shadow of a doubt *"that I am the LORD."*

Ezekiel 38:23 proclaims this being done by the supernatural destruction of the Antichrist, and even all the mighty armies that are with him, which will be destruction and death never before equaled.

The words *"magnify Myself"* and *"sanctify Myself"* have terrifying consequences if used in the negative.

It has reference to anger held in check for a long time and then exploding with a fury that defies description. It pertains to the honoring of His name, especially after the Antichrist has blasphemed the Lord for a period of some seven years.

The phrase, *"I will be known in the eyes of many nations,"* refers to this that will be done as described, which, no doubt, will be portrayed all over the world by television actually as it is happening.

Therefore, not only will the Antichrist be defeated, but due to these actions by the Lord, the entirety of the world will instantly know and recognize His power, glory, and majesty. The Scripture says that He will come back *"King of kings, and Lord of lords"* (Rev. 19:16).

Then, beyond a shadow of a doubt, let us say it again, *"They shall know that I am the* LORD.*"*

This will begin the glorious kingdom age, with Christ reigning personally and supreme from Jerusalem.

THE BATTLE OF ARMAGEDDON

"Therefore, you son of man, prophesy against Gog, and say, Thus says the Lord GOD; *Behold, I am against you, O Gog, the chief prince of Meshech and Tubal"* (Ezek. 39:1).

As is overly obvious, the Lord is against the Antichrist; therefore, anything the Lord is against cannot ultimately come out to success irrespective of how strong it may seem to be at the beginning.

The Antichrist will think that his attack on Israel is of his making, but the truth is, it is the Lord who will engineer these events.

This prophecy was given about 2,500 years ago, proclaiming the omniscience of the Lord in that He knows all things—past, present, and future. What a mighty God we serve!

I AM AGAINST YOU, O GOG

The Lord says in this verse, *"Behold, I am against you, O Gog,"* and this proclaims in these simple words the doom of the Man of Sin.

Ezekiel 36 told of Israel's coming restoration, with Ezekiel 37 saying how it would be done (by the Spirit of God). Ezekiel 38 portrays Satan's opposition to the Spirit of God, and this time through the Antichrist, called Gog. This chapter proclaims Gog's defeat by the Lord Jesus Christ. It is the battle of Armageddon as described in Revelation 16:16.

Plainly the Lord says, *"I am against you, O Gog."*

As previously stated, the phrase, *"The chief prince of Meshech and Tubal,"* has no reference to any particular locality but, instead, refers to the great confederation of Gentile nations throwing in their lot with the Antichrist in order to destroy Israel.

One of the reasons the phrase is used accordingly is because Gog, the Antichrist, is a Jew, and at least in these circumstances, it is somewhat strange for Gentile armies to follow a Jew, especially as he attempts to destroy his own people.

Even though there is no particular Scripture that specifically states that the Antichrist will be Jewish, still, it is virtually impossible that the Jews would proclaim as Messiah anyone who is not Jewish. At the beginning, they will think this man is the Messiah (Jn. 5:43).

THE NORTH PARTS

"And I will turn you back, and leave but the sixth part of you, and will cause you to come up from the north parts, and will bring you upon the mountains of Israel" (Ezek. 39:2).

Some Bible teachers claim that Ezekiel 38 and 39 pertain to another battle other than the battle of Armageddon, but a proper interpretation of the Scripture plainly shows that this individual, who is the Antichrist, is going to make a concentrated effort against Israel. Needless to say, this is far more than a police action but is, instead, a wholesale invasion of the land. Also, the manner in which he will be opposed by the Lord, once again, proclaims this as the battle of Armageddon. The fact that Israel is wondrously restored after this plainly portrays this as the final and concluding conflict.

Immediately after Ezekiel 39, the total restoration of the land, with the construction of the temple, is given to us in minute detail, which further portrays this conflict as the final one and, therefore, the battle of Armageddon.

This portrayal in these two chapters could not portray the invasion of the Antichrist some three and one-half years earlier when he will break his seven-year covenant with Israel (Dan. 9:27). This is because that particular conflict, which will happen before the battle of Armageddon, will be somewhat incomplete simply because the Antichrist will be threatened by other enemies out of the north and east according to Daniel 11:44.

At the end of these three and one-half years of subduing these enemies and preparing for the total annihilation of Israel, who will have filtered back into the land during the absence of the Antichrist, he is now prepared for this final conflict. It will be fought on the field of Megiddo and is called by the Lord "Armageddon" (Rev. 16:16).

THE SIXTH PART

Due to the fact that God is almighty, there is no way that any army or conglomeration of armies can defeat the Lord.

Still, the incurable heart of man that is grossly deceived, even as the heart of the Antichrist will be grossly deceived, thinks that God can be circumvented, ignored, or even defeated. However, it will not happen, as it cannot happen.

This great conflict will signal the second coming, which will portray the Lord as a man of war. As previously stated, the prophet Zechariah said, *"Then* (at this battle) *shall the LORD go forth, and fight against those nations, as when He fought in the day of battle"* (Zech. 14:3).

At this time, and due to the Lord fighting against the Man of Sin, the entirety of his armies will be destroyed with the exception of a sixth part. How large his army will be, we aren't told; however, it, no doubt, will include many hundreds of thousands of men, possibly even a million or more. At any rate, when it's all over, only one out of six will remain alive.

This we do know: so many men will be killed that blood will flow for a space of about 184 miles to the horses' bridles, which is about 5 or 6 feet deep.

Actually, the Scripture does not say that this deluge will be all blood but, instead calls it *"the winepress,"* which, no doubt, denotes the *"overflowing rain"* of Ezekiel 38:22 mixed with blood (Rev. 14:20).

THE ROUTE OF THE INVASION

"And I will turn you back, and leave but the sixth part of you, and will cause you to come up from the north parts, and will bring you upon the mountains of Israel" (Ezek. 39:2). This verse refers

to the Lord bringing the Antichrist to this place, despite the fact that the Man of Sin will think that all of this is his idea.

As we have previously alluded, many Bible students have concluded that the phrase, *"To come up from the north parts,"* refers to Russia; however, this statement has no reference to Russia but instead refers to the invasion route being the same as it was for the Assyrians, Babylonians, Grecians, and others in the past.

In fact, many have taught that Ezekiel 38 and 39 portray some type of battle between Russia and Israel, therefore, claiming that this is not a description of the battle of Armageddon. However, the fall and, thereby, destruction of Soviet communism put that myth to rest. No, these two chapters describe the battle of Armageddon, and for the reasons that we have already given.

THE WORD OF THE LORD

"And I will smite your bow out of your left hand, and will cause your arrows to fall out of your right hand" (Ezek. 39:3). The emphasis of this verse is the pronoun *I*. It is used accordingly in these passages regarding the destruction of the Antichrist, denoting the fact that the Lord will be his opposer.

While the Antichrist, called Gog, will think he is fighting Israel only, in truth, he is fighting the Lord, a battle that he cannot hope to win. In fact, all should know and understand this great truth.

The Lord has never lost a battle, and the Lord will never lose a battle, irrespective of how small or how large it might be.

Bringing this into the realm of personal experiences of individual Christians, a tremendous truth should be well understood.

The Christian should find out what the Lord is doing, which can be done if self-will is laid aside and one ardently seeks the Lord, asking for leading and guidance. God uses men, and by that we mean both men and women. So, all believers should ascertain whom the Lord is truly using and place their support accordingly. However, there is a catch to all of this that most Christians don't seem to understand.

THE OPPOSITION OF SATAN

That which the Lord has truly called and is truly using will always be opposed greatly by Satan. Unfortunately, it seems that most Christians look for that which is never opposed, thinking that somehow signals the blessings of the Lord. It doesn't!

How many modern Christians would have thrown in their lot with Moses, with him spending 40 years at the back side of the desert? I can assure you that there are not many!

How many would have thrown in their lot with David when he was being hunted by Saul, a period of time that lasted for probably about 15 years? How many would have thrown in with Job when he lost everything he had, with even his so-called dearest friends blaming him for the tragedy and even his wife telling him that he should curse God and die? What about Paul when he languished in prison for several years, even during the prime of his ministry?

Going back to David, how many would have thrown in their lot with him when he was fleeing Absalom with basically the entirety of Israel turning against him? However, despite David's terrible sin, which he paid for dearly, such did not alter God's call on his heart and life. *"For the gifts and calling of God are without repentance"* (Rom. 11:29). This means that these callings and gifts are not subject to a change of mind on God's part.

This definitely doesn't mean that God condones sin in any fashion. God forbid! However, it does mean, as with David, that if there is a problem, and it is clearly repented of, the call of God is still there and is meant to be carried out. Whenever fellow Christians try to hinder that call, they are inviting disaster for themselves. Instead, they should do as the few did who tried to help David and, in fact, did help him, and they were greatly blessed by God (II Sam. 17:27-29). The notes concerning this in the Expositor's Study Bible say this: *"Three men brought these gifts—Shobi, Machir, and Barzillai. At a time like this, for anyone to say, 'I love you' is a blessing that can only be understood if one has walked where David walked. The Holy Spirit was so gracious as to record the kindness of these men. He will likewise record for eternity the kindness of all those who will stand by 'God's anointed.'"*

Even now, despite the fact that Israel is a long way from God, still, those who bless Israel, in whatever capacity, will be blessed by God, and then conversely, those who try to hurt Israel will be cursed by God, a position where no sane person desires to find himself (Gen. 12:3).

OPPOSITION

While opposition by other Christians to the true man of God in such situations may hurt the one opposed, it will not stop God's man or woman. At the same time, such ultimately will definitely fall out to hurt, even great hurt, for the opposer.

It seems that all of the nations of the world at the time of the battle of Armageddon will throw in their lot with the Antichrist or else remain neutral. In other words, it seems that none will side with Israel; nevertheless, the Lord will side with Israel, and that's all that really matters in any case.

THE COMPLETE DEFEAT

"You shall fall upon the mountains of Israel, you, and all your bands, and the people that is with you: I will give you unto the ravenous birds of every sort, and to the beasts of the field to be devoured" (Ezek. 39:4). The phrase in this verse, *"You shall fall upon the mountains of Israel,"* speaking of the Antichrist, is a prediction now given about 2,500 years ago but most assuredly one that will come to pass.

The idea of Ezekiel 39:4 is that the defeat of the Antichrist and his armies will be so severe that vultures and beasts will feed upon the multitudes of dead bodies littering the mountains of Israel.

The phrase, *"You shall fall,"* signifies not only the defeat of the Man of Sin but also the collapse of corrupt human society, which includes corrupt human government.

Man has ever attempted to rebuild the garden of Eden but without the Tree of Life, which is symbolic of the Lord Jesus Christ. His efforts have been in vain because it is impossible to do such; however, the grandest effort of all will be in the near future when the Antichrist will make his debut for world dominion—power over economies, governments, militaries, religions, and societies. Hence, at this time, *"His number is six hundred three-score and six."* It is *"the number of a man,"* denoting man's supreme effort while at the same time denoting man's inherent weakness (Rev. 13:18).

THE SECOND COMING

The second coming of the Lord will usher in true government, which will be upon the shoulder of Christ, referring to Him bearing the responsibility and, therefore, guaranteeing its success. The Tree of Life will be back in the garden, so to speak, and Paradise will finally be brought back—but only upon the advent of Christ.

In Ezekiel 39:4, the phrase *"and the people that is with you"* proclaims the somber note that not only will the Antichrist be destroyed but, as well, all who have thrown in their lot with him, proclaiming that they have made a bad choice. To fight against that which belongs to God is to fight against God! This is truth that most seem to never learn.

In fact, untold millions in the world will actually think that the Antichrist is some type of deity and will worship him accordingly, worship which the Antichrist will ardently seek.

YOU SHALL FALL

"You shall fall upon the open field: for I have spoken it, says the Lord GOD" (Ezek. 39:5).

The phrase, *"open field,"* refers to the time of the defeat of the Antichrist. It will be in the very midst of the battle, with the Antichrist bearing down on Jerusalem, thinking that victory is within his grasp (Zech. 14:1–3). In fact, he will have excellent reason to believe such simply because all of Israel will have been taken by the Man of Sin, and half of Jerusalem will fall as well. So, as far as he is concerned, at this particular time, he is only hours away from total victory (Zech. 14:2).

At the time when he is strongest, he will be destroyed, for *"I have spoken it, says the Lord GOD."*

THE FIRE ON MAGOG

"And I will send a fire on Magog, and among them who dwell carelessly in the isles: and they shall know that I am the LORD" (Ezek. 39:6). This verse simply means that the Lord will personally use the elements of the heavens to destroy the vast Gentile armies following the Antichrist.

The phrase, *"And among them who dwell carelessly in the isles,"* refers to other nations of the world, which in their minds are neutral and are simply turning a blind eye to this wholesale slaughter against Israel by the Antichrist. During the late 1930s and at the outset of World War II, many nations of the world, including the United States, knew what was taking place regarding the Jews but still did nothing about it; consequently, 6 million Jews were slaughtered by the demon-possessed madmen of Hitlerite Germany. Finally, America did wake up, as well as other countries, but not in time to stop the slaughter.

Whereas there was somewhat of a reprieve extended by the Lord concerning that encounter, there will be no reprieve concerning this final encounter. Every nation will be held accountable. Every nation *"shall know that I am the LORD."*

In the late 1930s, the Lord said little and did little; however, at the time of the coming battle of Armageddon, He is going to say much and do much!

In fact, the entirety of the world at that time *"shall know that I am the LORD."*

TELEVISION

As we have already alluded, it is positive that every major television news network in the world will be represented at the battle of Armageddon. The Antichrist, the egomaniac that he will be, will want the entirety of the world to see his great victory as he annihilates Israel. No doubt, he has plans, which will have already been formulated, for the greatest gala event the world has ever known—his enthronement as the king of kings and lord of lords. To be sure, it will look as if he is going to pull it off.

On a constant basis, news reports will come in from the battlefront, with television coverage of his advance going into billions of homes around the world. Steadily, his gigantic army will crowd Jerusalem, with news reports going out constantly that victory is near. In fact, half the city will fall (Zech. 14:2).

However, the prophet Zechariah also predicted that when it looks as if it's all over; when it looks as if the Antichrist will do what Haman, Herod, and Hitler could not do; when it looks as if Satan is just about ready to administer the final blow; and when it looks as if these ancient people, Israel, are about to die—that's when a strange phenomenon in the heavens could very well happen. Jesus said:

> *For as the lightning cometh out of the east, and shineth even unto the west; so shall also the coming of the Son of Man be .... Immediately after the tribulation of those days shall the sun be darkened, and the moon shall not give her light, and the stars shall fall from heaven, and the powers of the heavens shall be shaken: and then shall appear the sign of the Son of Man in heaven* (Mat. 24:27, 29–30).

EVERY EYE SHALL SEE HIM

Media crews will point their television cameras toward the heavens, thinking that the Antichrist is about to introduce a new type of weapon. In fact, hundreds, if not thousands, of newscasters may very well be attempting to explain this great phenomenon to all the people of the world, possibly stating that what the Antichrist is now introducing will surely mean the finish of Israel.

But then, the terminology will change. It is quite possible that the newscasters, in their attempt to explain this phenomenon to the world, will exclaim something like this: "Is it possible? Can it be? Ladies and gentlemen, see for yourselves. Millions of white horses, each one carrying a rider with a startling glory like we've never seen. And there is one leading them, and His glory is such as has never been witnessed before. And yes, He has a banner stretched around His body with a name written on it: King of kings and Lord of lords! Could it be? Is it Jesus Christ?"

The Scripture says, *"Behold, He comes with clouds* (clouds of saints); *and every eye shall see Him, and they also which pierced Him"* (Rev. 1:7).

The phrase, *"every eye shall see Him,"* could refer to those in Israel, and especially in the vicinity of Jerusalem. However, due to modern communications, it probably has reference to most of the world, which could only be carried out by television, to which we have alluded.

HIS COMING

When He came the first time, He came as a lowly human being, raised in the home of peasant parents, in which Isaiah prophesied, *"And when we shall see Him, there is no beauty that we should desire Him"* (Isa. 53:2).

In fact, at the conclusion of His life and ministry, He was spit upon, laughed at, caricatured, beaten, ostracized, ridiculed, lampooned, and put on a cross. But when He comes back the second time, it will be totally different. He will come back in such glory as the world has never known before, and as the Scripture has said, *"crowned King of kings and Lord of lords."* In other words, the second coming will be the most cataclysmic event by far that the world has ever known. There has been nothing in history that could even remotely compare with this, which the Bible proclaims.

When you consider that every saint of God who has ever lived will come back with Christ, all with glorified bodies, such will stagger the imagination.

Millions ask the question, Will this really happen? The answer is simple: If He came the first time, and He most definitely did, then for certain He will come the second time (Rev. 19).

Will your anchor hold in the storms of life,
When the clouds unfold their wings of strife?
When the strong tides lift, and the cables strain,
Will your anchor drift or firm remain?

It is safely moored, 'twill the storm withstand,
For 'tis well secured by the Savior's hand;
And the cables, passed from His heart to mine,
Can defy that blast, through strength divine.

It will firmly hold in the straits of fear,
When the breakers have told the reef is near;
Though the tempest rave and the wild winds blow,
Not an angry wave shall our bark o'erflow.

It will surely hold in the floods of death,
When the waters cold chill our latest breath;
On the rising tide it can never fail,
While our hopes abide within the veil.

When our eyes behold through the gathering night,
The city of gold, our harbor bright,
We shall anchor fast by the heavenly shore,
With the storms all past forevermore.

CHAPTER 6

I WILL MAKE MY HOLY NAME KNOWN

I WILL MAKE MY HOLY NAME KNOWN

"SO WILL I MAKE MY holy name known in the midst of My people Israel; and I will not let them pollute My holy name anymore: and the heathen shall know that I am the LORD, *the Holy One in Israel"* (Ezek. 39:7). This verse captures all the promises made by the Lord to the patriarchs and prophets of old. It is as if the Lord has been asleep but suddenly awakens.

IT IS DONE

Making His name known in the midst of His people Israel will be done in different ways.

There has been no moving or operation of the Holy Spirit in Israel or among Jews for nearly 2,000 years. This certainly does not mean that individual Jews have not been saved because some have come to Christ down through the centuries. However, that was all on an individual basis and had little to do with the great promises given to the patriarchs and prophets of old.

Therefore, the fulfillment of this promise will be basically in two forms:

1. The salvation of the 144,000 (Rev. 7); the two witnesses (Rev. 11:3–13).
2. The second coming of the Lord (Rev. 19).

While the other things play a very important part, still, it is the second coming that will open the eyes of Israel and, in fact, the entirety of the world.

THE POLLUTION OF THE NAME
OF THE LORD HAS ENDED

Ezekiel 39:7 continues, *"and I will not let them pollute My holy name any more."*

For a period of some seven years, the Antichrist will, in fact, greatly pollute the name of the Lord. He will actually declare war on the Lord Jesus Christ, and do so in varied ways. Where he has any power at all, He will confiscate every Bible and demand total allegiance to himself, plus have a hatred for Christ.

Furthermore, the Scripture says, *"And there was given unto him a mouth speaking great things and blasphemies."* It also says, *"And he opened his mouth in blasphemy against God, to blaspheme His name, and His tabernacle, and them who dwell in heaven"* (Rev. 13:5–6).

But at the second coming of the Lord, the pollution will end once and for all.

THE ENTIRETY OF THE WORLD WILL KNOW

The last phrase of Ezekiel 39:7, *"And the heathen shall know that I am the* LORD, *the Holy One in Israel,"* will proclaim once and for all that Jesus Christ is Lord. These very prophecies in Ezekiel, plus the other prophecies, are little believed by the world. Even much of the church no longer believes that Israel has any part in the great plan of God. However, this passage, plus many others, tells us differently.

At the second coming of the Lord, to which these passages refer, so dramatic will be the Lord's rescue of Israel that the world will have absolutely no doubt as to who Israel's Saviour is.

As stated, the second coming of Christ will be televised by a multitude of camera crews standing by to broadcast on various networks the great victory of the Antichrist. Instead, they will record the great victory of the Lord Jesus Christ.

At the time of this writing, more than 6 billion people in this world have access to a television set or a media device of some kind. They will be eagerly watching the events in the Middle East unfold, only they will see and hear far more than they could have ever imagined.

As we have done our best to describe, they will see the second coming of Christ, which will be the most dramatic event that has ever happened in human history. Then the heathen shall know.

THIS IS THE DAY

"Behold, it is come, and it is done, says the LORD GOD; *this is the day whereof I have spoken"* (Ezek. 39:8). This verse pertains to the coming great tribulation period and to the events surrounding that era. Even though these words were spoken

approximately 2,500 years ago, they are so certain of fulfillment that the Holy Spirit says through the prophet, *"It is done."* As someone has said, "Read the last page of the book—we win!"

The events leading up to this time, which, in effect, is the very time in which we are now living, are proclaimed by the Scriptures as being a time of spiritual declension.

Economically and numerically, the American church has never been stronger, but, spiritually speaking, it is at its lowest ebb since the Reformation. Churches are being filled with people clamoring to hear a social message. In fact, the most popular of all is the self-improvement message. The tragedy is that none of this is the gospel of Jesus Christ, but rather a Band-Aid that is being placed over the cancer of sin, with the end result being, as always, acute destruction. The real problem in mankind, as it has always been the real problem, is sin, but the modern church acts as if sin does not exist, with the subject being little broached, except in a nebulous way. All the while, the bondages of darkness are taking their deadly toll. Not only is this Band-Aid of social gospel not helping the people, but it's also severely harming them.

THE SEEKER SENSITIVE MODE

Some years back I heard an interview of the man who began the seeker sensitive movement. He was asked how his church—a church that supposedly runs 25,000 or 30,000 people—had its beginning.

His team had taken surveys, he said, of people living within a radius of several miles or so of the locations where they had thought about planting a church. From those surveys, they found out that the people did not want to hear anything about sin, nothing about hell, nothing about the cross, nothing about the crucifixion of Christ, and nothing about the shed blood of the Lamb. They wanted to be made to feel good. So that's what they gave the people, he said, and that's the reason why his church became so large.

Sometime later I read in a particular religious magazine an interview that this same man had given concerning a poll that had been taken in his church. He said in this poll, the people responding did not have to sign their names and could therefore be honest with their answers.

He said, "I found that our church was filled with alcoholics, drug addicts, fornicators, child molesters, and just about everything you could name."

These results were not at all what his team thought they would be. He said they were going to have to rethink their situation and come up with another strategy.

But the answer to his situation is very simple: He needs to preach Jesus Christ and Him crucified. He needs to warn men about hell because most in his church, if not all, are going there unless they give their hearts to Christ. He needs to weep over the lost, and he needs to preach Jesus Christ and the cross as the only answer for the ills of man. That means he needs to preach the blood, and above all, he needs to preach the cross of Christ. Man's problem is sin, and the solution to that problem is the cross of Christ. I might quickly add that the cross of Christ is the *only* solution to man's problem.

LET'S LOOK AT THE CROSS

Man's problem is sin, whether he's redeemed or otherwise, and the only solution for sin or anything that addresses itself to humankind is the cross of Christ.

Tragedy of tragedies, the cross isn't being preached at all, with some few remote exceptions. Satan does everything within his power to cover up or sidetrack the true solution. Tragically, he succeeds by and large with much of the modern church.

The theme for one of Crossfire's International Youth Conferences was "Breaking the Sin Cycle." My grandson, Gabriel Swaggart, heads up Crossfire, our local youth group, which sponsors this annual conference held at Family Worship Center. Gabriel said that the Lord gave that title to him. His message on the Friday night of that particular conference proclaimed the solution to the terrible sin cycle, which alone is the cross. I was thrilled as I watched the Lord anoint him to proclaim this message, and to do so in no uncertain terms, which resulted in the altars being filled with young people.

Before it is too late, we must preach the cross! We must proclaim the cross! We must hold it up as the only answer to a hurting and dying world (Rom. 5:1; 6:3–14; 8:1–2, 11; I Cor. 1:17–18, 21, 23; 2:2; Col. 2:10-15).

I WILL DRAW ALL MEN UNTO ME

Jesus said, *"And I, if I be lifted up from the earth, will draw all men unto Me. This He said, signifying what death He should die"*

(Jn. 12:32–33). As is obvious in this verse, Christ being lifted up from the earth has to do with Him being lifted up on the cross. That and that alone, which paid the price for man's terrible sin problem, can set the captive free.

The phrase of Ezekiel 39:8, *"This is the day whereof I have spoken,"* pertains to the coming great tribulation period, and more especially to these events at the very conclusion of that particular time.

It pertains to the actual day of the battle of Armageddon, which will, in fact, last only one day (Zech. 14:7). However, this only speaks of the day of the coming of the Lord and does not refer to the many months of preparation for the battle or other parts of the conflicts that will precede this momentous day.

SEVEN YEARS

"And they who dwell in the cities of Israel shall go forth, and shall set on fire and burn the weapons, both the shields and the bucklers, the bows and the arrows, and the handstaves, and the spears, and they shall burn them with fire seven years" (Ezek. 39:9). Concerning the weapons that will litter the battlefield, this verse says, *"and they shall burn them with fire seven years."*

Most weapons are made of iron, steel, or other types of metals. Still, there will be enough combustible material to keep a contingency of people appointed for this very task busy for some seven years. From this we know that this army of the Antichrist is going to be hundreds of thousands—if not millions—strong. As well, five-sixths of that army will perish at the second coming of the Lord.

As we have said previously, in giving this to Ezekiel concerning events that have not yet come to pass, the Holy Spirit used names for weaponry that were common in those days. Had he used modern names, such as tanks or fighter jets, Bible scholars would not have known what was being discussed. So, and rightly so, names were used that were common then and are very understandable now.

THE VICTORS

"So that they shall take no wood out of the field, neither cut down any out of the forests; for they shall burn the weapons with fire: and they shall spoil those who spoiled them, and rob those who robbed them, says the Lord GOD" (Ezek. 39:10). This verse refers to the Antichrist coming to an ignominious end, in fact, the very opposite of that which he had planned.

In the so-called "Peace for Galilee" campaign, when Israel attempted to destroy the PLO, I was invited with several of my associates to Israel where we would be taken into Lebanon at the very height of the conflict. This happened in 1983, if I remember correctly, and it was the closest to war that I had ever come.

Of all the things seen and experienced, the mile after mile of Israeli tractor-trailers hauling back captured equipment, both damaged and undamaged, was a scene I will not soon forget. Some of the battle tanks looked as if they had been opened with a giant can opener, while others seemed to be untouched. As well, there were myriad truckloads of other captured war material, which, if usable, was placed in Israel's inventory. At any rate, the amount was staggering, which gives one an idea as to the fulfillment of Ezekiel 39:10. Whereas the armies just mentioned only numbered tens of thousands, the armies of the Antichrist will number hundreds of thousands, if not many millions.

So, if one could multiply what I witnessed those years ago by a thousand, one would have an idea of what is meant by these predictions.

Much, if not most, of the weaponry of the world will be gathered at this battle of Armageddon.

WEAPONS

At the time of this writing, and what is little known by the rest of the world is that Saudi Arabia has developed several underground bases in their vast land. They contain the very latest in technological military equipment, with much, if not most, purchased from America and costing nearly half a trillion dollars.

For what does Saudi Arabia need such a vast array of the most technologically advanced equipment? She need have no fear from Israel but probably fears most her own fellow Arabs!

However, the likelihood of a conflict between Arab states, at least of this magnitude, is unlikely; therefore, it is a definite possibility that this vast array of weaponry will fall into the hands of the coming Antichrist. Daniel said, *"But he shall have power over the treasures of gold and of silver"* (Dan. 11:43). Of course, this which gold and silver can buy will definitely be included.

GOG

"And it shall come to pass in that day, that I will give unto Gog a place there of graves in Israel, the valley of the passengers on the east of the sea: and it shall stop the noses of the passengers: and there shall they bury Gog and all his multitude: and they shall call it The valley of Hamongog" (Ezek. 39:11). This verse proclaims the fact that Israel will be the grave of the Antichrist and, in fact, all his armies instead of the place of victory he had so surely thought it would be.

Down through the centuries, battle after battle has been fought in the land of Israel. The conflict has been almost unceasing for the last 3,500 years, but this will be the last conflict and will, in fact, be the greatest of them all. It will be a conflict totally different from any that has ever been waged at that particular place, or anywhere else for that matter.

While Israel will definitely be a participant, it will be the coming of the Lord and the way in which He will fight—a manner that He has not fought since days of old—that will decide this conflict, and do so in no uncertain terms (Zech. 14:3).

On that great day of battle, among all the dead will be Gog—the Antichrist. His death will herald the demise of Satan's greatest and final effort to usurp authority over Christ. At this time Christ will bind Satan with a *"great chain"* and *"cast him into the bottomless pit, and shut him up, and set a seal upon him, that he should deceive the nations no more, till the thousand years should be fulfilled: and after that he must be loosed a little season,"* which will, no doubt, also include all fallen angels and demon spirits (Rev. 20:1–3).

The phrase, *"And they shall call it The valley of Hamongog,"* refers to the valley of Megiddo, which will be called, at least for a time, "The multitude of Gog." It actually will refer to the multitude slain by God at this great occasion.

The skeptic and unbeliever would have nothing but criticism for the actions of the Lord regarding the deaths of so many in this momentous conflict; however, such will come about only after repeated efforts by the Lord to solicit repentance, but to no avail (Rev. 9:20–21).

The destruction will be an act of much needed surgery because it will be against those who have vowed the destruction of God and all that belongs to Him. As well, they are the ones who will have taken peace from the earth and, thereby, caused the suffering and deaths of untold hundreds of millions.

Only those who desire unrighteousness and, thereby, further pain and suffering would take exception to these happenings. At last the question, *"How long?"* will be answered (Rev. 6:10).

HOW DOES SATAN THINK HE CAN DEFEAT THE LORD?

The Lord is almighty, meaning that He can do anything and is, in fact, the Creator who has created all things (Jn. 1:1–3). Satan is but a creature, meaning that in eternity past, Lucifer, the great angel, was created by God and, of course, was created in righteousness and holiness. At some point in time, he led a revolution against God, which has raged from then until now. For all practical purposes, the battle of Armageddon will be Satan's swan song.

While it is true that he will be loosed a little season from the bottomless pit where he will be incarcerated for a thousand years, along with all demon spirits and fallen angels, his efforts at that time will be short lived (Rev. 20:1–10).

When we speak of Satan attempting to usurp authority over God and, in fact, defeat Him, there is only one way that Satan can hope to gain his devious ends. Of course, all the Lord has to do is say the word, and Satan is no more. The reason He hasn't done this before now is actually a mystery, but this we do know: The Lord has His reasons for everything, and to be sure, He does all things well. So, His allowing Satan to continue for this period of time has been for good reason, which eternity future will reveal its wisdom.

THE WORD OF THE LORD

The only way that Satan could ever think of defeating the Lord is by Satan stopping the Word of the Lord from coming to pass. This he has repeatedly tried to do, even from the very beginning. As stated, his greatest effort will be the Antichrist, and especially the battle of Armageddon.

If he can defeat Israel, then all the many promises made by the Lord as it regards this ancient people will fall to the ground, and, in effect, Satan will have won the conflict, with God being dethroned and Satan taking His place. Of course, we know that cannot happen, but Satan is so deceived that he actually believes he can win the day.

In fact, the Word of the Lord, and we speak of the Bible, is of such significance that the Scripture says, *"For You have magnified Your Word above all Your name"* (Ps. 138:2).

So, everything hinges on the Word of the Lord. That's why Jesus also said, *"For verily I say unto you, Till heaven and earth pass, one jot or one tittle shall in no wise pass from the law, till all be fulfilled"* (Mat. 5:18).

SEVEN MONTHS

"And seven months shall the house of Israel be burying of them, that they may cleanse the land" (Ezek. 39:12).

Of course, modern equipment could accomplish this task in a few days; however, the latter phrase, *"That they may cleanse the land,"* refers to every bone being found and gathered, which will take seven months.

All of this means that there will not be a single bone left in the land, but it will be found and put in a particular place. In other words, the land must be cleansed as it regards this battle, and to be sure, the land will be cleansed.

THE LORD WILL BE GLORIFIED

"Yes, all the people of the land shall bury them; and it shall be to them a renown the day that I shall be glorified, says the Lord God"

(Ezek. 39:13). As it regards gathering every bone, this verse links this spectacle to the sanctifying of the name of the Lord.

Normally, the Lord sanctifies His name by love freely offered and freely received, but if instead it is spurned and blasphemously denounced, His name is sanctified and glorified by judgment. Therefore, all men will answer to God in one way or the other, whether by mercy and grace or by judgment, but answer they shall.

CLEANSING THE LAND

"And they shall sever out men of continual employment, passing through the land to bury with the passengers those who remain upon the face of the earth, to cleanse it: after the end of seven months shall they search" (Ezek. 39:14).

The phrase in this verse, *"those who remain,"* indicates that at least some of the sixth part left of the armies of the Antichrist will be employed in this effort of cleansing the land. In fact, it would stand to reason that this is certain.

After seeing and experiencing the second coming of Jesus Christ—the most powerful portrayal of His majesty and might— many of the remaining army of the Antichrist will more than likely turn to the Lord.

A CONTINUED CLEANSING

"And the passengers who pass through the land, when any sees a man's bone, then shall he set up a sign by it, till the buriers have

buried it in the valley of Hamongog" (Ezek. 39:15). This verse indicates that the battle area will cover large parts of Israel, with the slain covering many miles, perhaps the entire length and breadth of Israel. Quite possibly, it could even spill over into surrounding countries.

It seems that all the bones will be collected and taken to the valley of Hamongog and there buried. If this is the case, it will be done for a reason—the portraying of such as a monument to Satan's defeat and the great victory of the Lord Jesus Christ.

THEY WILL CLEANSE THE LAND

"And also the name of the city shall be Hamonah. Thus shall they cleanse the land" (Ezek. 39:16).

With the attention given to the cleansing of the land, it is obvious that this is something the Holy Spirit fervently desires. In fact, this will be the last battle fought for 1,000 years, and that speaks of the entirety of the earth.

Now think about that for a moment: No more war, no more killing, no more wasting of earth's resources upon conflict— no more.

What did the great prophet Isaiah say about this? He said, *"And He shall judge among the nations, and shall rebuke many people: and they shall beat their swords into plowshares, and their spears into pruninghooks: nation shall not lift up sword against nation, neither shall they learn war anymore"* (Isa. 2:4).

When Jesus was refused by Israel, even though He offered them the kingdom, this subjected the entirety of the world for now some 2,000 years more of war and rumors of war. Concerning this, He said, *"And you shall hear of wars and rumors of wars ... For nation shall rise against nation, and kingdom against kingdom: and there shall be famines, and pestilences, and earthquakes, in divers places. All these are the beginning of sorrows"* (Mat. 24:6-8).

There will be no war during the coming kingdom age simply because Jesus, the Prince of Peace, will be present constantly on this earth. In fact, He will govern the entirety of the world in one way or the other as King of kings and Lord of lords.

For the first time in its history, planet Earth will know peace and prosperity as never before. Hunger will be eradicated. False religions will have no more place. Satan and all of his fallen angels and demon spirits will be locked away in the bottomless pit. What a day that will be! The glorious thing about it is that it's not going to be very long until all of this is going to come to pass. We are now living in the closing days of the church age, which means the rapture of the church could take place at any time. Then the world will be plunged into great tribulation, greater than it has ever known before. Satan will then make his greatest debut yet in the form of the Antichrist, which will plunge this world into war as never before. To be sure, Satan would have his way but for one thing, and that one thing is the greatest happening the world will have ever known. It will be the second coming of Jesus Christ, which will be the most cataclysmic event the world has ever experienced.

THE DEFEAT OF THE ANTICHRIST

"And, you son of man, thus says the Lord GOD; *Speak unto every feathered fowl, and to every beast of the field, Assemble yourselves, and come; gather yourselves on every side to My sacrifice that I do sacrifice for you, even a great sacrifice upon the mountains of Israel, that you may eat flesh, and drink blood"* (Ezek. 39:17). The words of Ezekiel are very similar to those of John as given to us in Revelation 19:17-18, 20. It also refers to the statement of Christ when He said, *"Wheresoever the carcass is, there will the eagles be gathered together"* (Mat. 24:28), and *"Wheresoever the body is, thither will the eagles be gathered together"* (Lk. 17:37). Actually the word *eagles* should have been translated *vultures*.

No doubt, due to the tremendous numbers who will be slaughtered, vultures and beasts will be engaged, as such is always the case. Still, the passage is meant to impress upon the reader the tremendous numbers that will be killed.

Even though the great sacrifice mentioned pertains to the slaughter of the army of the Antichrist, it also points to the sacrifice of Christ at Calvary, which was rejected. Therefore, the lesson should not be lost on the reader that if the sacrifice of Christ is rejected, the individual(s) will ultimately become a sacrifice himself, but a sacrifice that will not save.

THE FLESH AND THE BLOOD

The apt description given, *"that you may eat flesh, and drink blood,"* is very similar to the statement made by Christ concerning Himself: *"Verily, verily, I say unto you, Except you eat the flesh of the Son of Man, and drink His blood, you have no life in you"* (Jn. 6:53).

The only answer for a hurting, dying, and satanically bound human race is the cross of Christ. It was there that Jesus Christ offered His body in sacrifice and thereby poured out His precious blood. This alone was and is able to set the captive free.

It simply refers to the believer evidencing faith in Christ and what Christ did at the cross. That is constituted as eating His flesh and drinking His blood.

Let the reader understand (as we have already alluded) that the sacrifice of Christ rejected means that the individual, nation, or group of nations, such as here represented, will themselves be a sacrifice. The latter will be a sacrifice that will not save, but rather will spell doom for all involved.

THE SACRIFICE OF CLEANSING

"You shall eat the flesh of the mighty, and drink the blood of the princes of the earth, of rams, of lambs, and of goats, of bullocks, all of them fatlings of Bashan" (Ezek. 39:18).

Let us say it again: This mighty army will have refused to eat the flesh and drink the blood of the Son of God, which refers to the price that He would pay at the cross in order that men might be saved. Instead, they will have their flesh eaten and their blood drunk by the fowls of the heavens.

Ezekiel 39:18 signifies the military and political elite of the army of the Antichrist.

The powerful confederation of forces gathered by the Antichrist had, no doubt, made plans for the subjugation of the entire world, with certain areas of the world already parceled out to these "mighty." The idea is that they have all, and without fail, been foiled by the coming of Christ. In addition to the Antichrist being killed, most, if not all, of his leaders will be killed.

For the first time, the world is going to see the Lord Jesus Christ as He actually is. In other words, when He comes back the second time, which He most definitely shall, He is not coming back to be laughed at, caricatured, lambasted, spit upon, and ultimately crucified. Rather, He is coming back with power such as the world has never known, seen, or witnessed before. To be sure, the whole world, including the Man of Sin and Satan himself, is going to see just how powerful that the Lord Jesus really is.

YOU WILL DRINK OF THE BLOOD

"And you shall eat fat till you be full, and drink blood till you be drunken, of My sacrifice which I have sacrificed for you" (Ezek. 39:19). This verse presents a startling statement. The idea is that if they would not accept the sacrifice of Christ at Calvary, then they would be made a sacrifice, but it would not save their souls. Instead, it would serve as a part of the sacrifice of cleansing, which means to cleanse the world of such evil.

The truth presented here concerning the sacrifice is so important that it is repeated again by the Holy Spirit. Christ died as a sacrifice to save humanity. All who receive that sacrifice unto themselves and have faith in its atoning offering will be saved (Jn. 3:16). But all who refuse to receive it have, in essence, set themselves against God and His plan for the human family. Therefore, they will be made a sacrifice themselves, as stipulated here, in order for the world to rid itself of its malignancy.

However, the sacrifice recorded here in no way saves the victim. Instead, it cleanses the world in order that the righteous may enjoy the blessings of God.

MY TABLE

"Thus you shall be filled at My table with horses and chariots, with mighty men, and with all men of war, says the Lord GOD" (Ezek. 39:20). This verse contains a wealth of information.

The Antichrist has made his plans for world dominion, and after some seven years of carnage, warfare, murder, and mayhem, he is well on his way to the realization of his goal.

The plans formulated by these demon-possessed sons of darkness no doubt include the death of every single person on the face of the earth who will not promise total allegiance to the Antichrist and total denial of the God of heaven. In other words, Gog is preparing a table of sacrifice for anyone on the earth who does not recognize him as god and offer him worship. But the second coming of the Lord will change the direction of this table. Instead of this son of darkness preparing a table, he will become a table, in effect, *"My table,"* which speaks of him being totally and completely defeated.

THE HEATHEN

"And I will set My glory among the heathen, and all the heathen shall see My judgment that I have executed, and My hand that I have laid upon them" (Ezek. 39:21). The phrase in this verse, *"And I will set My glory among the heathen,"* pertains to all who do not know the Lord, whomever they might be, and wherever they might be.

The Bible regards all who do not accept the Lord Jesus Christ as their Saviour as *"the heathen,"* and that includes almost all of the world.

In effect, every single person in so-called Christian America, as well as any place else in the world, who does not know the Lord Jesus Christ as his personal Saviour is regarded by the Lord as heathen. Living in a country such as America, which adheres, at least somewhat, to the principle of Christianity, in no way changes the status of the individual person. Only the acceptance of Christ as one's Saviour will change this designation as given by the Holy Spirit.

As well, the idea is put forth that the Antichrist had planned to set his glory over the entire world, but, instead, Christ will set His glory among the heathen.

The phrase, *"and all the heathen shall see My judgment that I have executed,"* refers to the entirety of the 1,000-year millennial reign when Christ will rule this world exclusively, and the government shall be upon His shoulder (Isa. 9:6–7). However, it includes most of the world actually seeing the second coming portrayed over television even as it happens.

THE LORD JESUS CHRIST

"So the house of Israel shall know that I am the LORD their God from that day and forward" (Ezek. 39:22).

Along with the heathen seeing this glorious spectacle, likewise, the house of Israel will now know exactly who the Messiah is. They will know that the one they rejected and crucified is actually the Lord their God. They will know it from that very day and forward. There will be no argument. His identity will be obvious specifically because of the nail prints in His hands.

The Scripture says, *"And one shall say unto Him, What are these wounds in Your hands? Then He shall answer, Those with which I was wounded in the house of My friends"* (Zech. 13:6).

As should be obvious, there is a note of sarcasm in the answer that will be given by our Lord, and rightly so.

CAPTIVITY

"And the heathen shall know that the house of Israel went into captivity for their iniquity: because they trespassed against Me, therefore hid I My face from them, and gave them into the hand of their enemies: so fell they all by the sword" (Ezek. 39:23).

At the time of the second coming, the entirety of the world will then know who is Lord. It could not be accomplished with mercy and grace, for Israel crucified that mercy and grace, so it will be accomplished with judgment.

Ezekiel 39:23 pertains to the entirety of the world being made aware and understanding exactly what has happened to

Israel. It was sin that caused Israel's destruction, and, to be sure, sin will place anyone in captivity.

THE SIN NATURE

The only way the sin cycle can be broken is by the sinner accepting Christ and making Him Lord and Saviour of his life.

Even then, and we refer to the post-conversion experience, if the believer doesn't maintain his faith in Christ and the cross, ever understanding that the cross is the means of our victory, the sin nature will once again rule in the believer's life, bringing untold difficulties and problems. Paul said concerning this very thing, *"Let not sin* (the sin nature) *therefore reign* (rule) *in your mortal body, that you should obey it in the lusts thereof"* (Rom. 6:12).

If there were no danger of this, as many teach, then the Holy Spirit through Paul wasted all of these instructions. Of course, we know that the Holy Spirit doesn't waste anything. In fact, He never minces words.

Some 17 times in Romans 6 alone, Paul mentions "sin." Fifteen times the definite article *the* is placed in front of the word *sin,* meaning *"the* sin," which actually refers to the sin nature. In other words, it's not speaking of particular acts of sin, but rather the principle of sin, or what causes people to sin.

One of the times, the word *sin* is used as a noun and not a verb, meaning that Paul is continuing to address himself to the sin nature (Rom. 6:14). So, that leaves only one time that refers to acts of sin (Rom. 6:15).

ROMANS 6

To counteract this monster, Paul begins his teaching in Romans 6 with an explanation of the cross (Rom. 6:3–5), and what it means to the person who has come to Christ. In other words, Paul tells us that sin is the problem (Rom. 6:1-2). He then takes us to the cross, which is the only cure for sin (Rom. 6:3-5).

Whenever a person comes to Christ, he is baptized into His death, buried with Him by baptism into death, and then raised with Him in newness of life. Please understand that Paul is not speaking here of water baptism, but rather our being baptized into Christ, which takes place in the mind of God when we give our hearts to Christ. In fact, there are three baptisms for believers:

1. *Baptism at conversion.* We are baptized into Christ at conversion. This is not a physical thing, but rather a spiritual thing (Rom. 6:3-5; Col. 2:10-15).

2. *Water baptism.* We are then baptized into water, which symbolizes our newfound life in Christ. Going under the water symbolizes our death, and we speak of being dead to sin, etc. Being raised out of the water proclaims one now having newness of life, i.e., resurrection life.

3. *Baptism with the Holy Spirit.* The baptism with the Holy Spirit is always accompanied by speaking with other tongues. While it is true that the Holy Spirit most definitely does come into the heart and life of all believing sinners at conversion, that is different than being

baptized with the Holy Spirit. At conversion, the Holy Spirit, one might say, baptizes us into Christ. At the Spirit baptism, Jesus baptizes us into the Spirit (Acts 2:4).

THE SANCTIFICATION CHAPTER

Romans 6 is the great sanctification chapter of the Bible. It is here that the Holy Spirit through Paul tells us how to live a victorious, overcoming Christian life. In other words, the sin nature must not have dominion over us (Rom. 6:14).

Paul begins with the cross, and, in fact, he never leaves the cross. It is the cross alone and our faith in that finished work of Christ that gives us victory over the world, the flesh, and the Devil (Col. 2:10–15). Otherwise, the believer will be in captivity to Satan in some way. The believer must understand that and, in fact, never forget it.

Be not dismayed whate'er betide,
God will take care of you;
Beneath His wings of love abide,
God will take care of you.

Through days of toil when heart doth fail,
God will take care of you;
When dangers fierce your path assail,
God will take care of you.

All you may need He will provide,
God will take care of you;
Nothing you ask will be denied,
God will take care of you.

No matter what may be the test,
God will take care of you;
Lean, weary one, upon His breast,
God will take care of you.

God will take care of you,
Through every day, o'er all the way;
He will take care of you,
God will take care of you.

CHAPTER 7

THE HIDDEN FACE
OF GOD

THE HIDDEN FACE OF GOD

"AND THE HEATHEN SHALL know that the house of Israel went into captivity for their iniquity: because they trespassed against Me, therefore hid I My face from them, and gave them into the hand of their enemies: so fell they all by the sword (Ezek. 39:23).

Looking at the experiences of Israel down through the many centuries, we know that the dispersions under the Assyrians, the Babylonians, and the Romans were all effected by the sword. As well, this pertains to all Jews who have been exiled through the centuries, and more particularly, the terrible Holocaust of World War II. All of this can justly be stated, *"so fell they all by the sword."*

The equity of God's action with Israel in all periods of their history—past, present, and future—is declared Ezekiel 39:22-29.

The phrase, *"they trespassed against Me,"* refers to Israel's rebellion from the very beginning, which finally necessitated their destruction and dispersion, which included the Babylonian captivity, as well as the destruction of Jerusalem by Titus in AD 70. However, the crowning trespass of all was their rejection of Christ and His crucifixion.

WE HAVE NO KING BUT CAESAR

They refused to believe their Messiah and our Lord and said, *"His blood be on us, and on our children"* (Mat. 27:25), and referring to His kingship, *"We have no king but Caesar"* (Jn. 19:15). As a result of their not wanting Him, *"Hid I My face from them."*

That lasted for nearly 2,000 years, with them being given over *"into the hand of their enemies."*

A PERSONAL EXPERIENCE

In the early 1980s, the Jewish community in the United States grew angry with me because I brought out these very things over our worldwide telecast. They were loath to admit that their terrible problems of the past and present were because of their rejection and crucifixion of Christ. I answered them as follows: "It is not that the Lord instituted the terrible persecutions that came upon the Jewish people down through the centuries but, instead, that they did not desire Him; therefore, He gave them into the hands of their enemies. It was not the Lord who did these things to them but their enemies." They did not want Him, so the only alternative was Caesar, and Caesar has been a hard taskmaster.

TRANSGRESSIONS

"According to their uncleanness and according to their transgressions have I done unto them, and hid My face from them" (Ezek. 39:24).

It is not that the Lord placed the demonic impulses in the madness of Adolf Hitler so that he would institute the Holocaust, but that he was the one that Israel chose instead of Christ. They made their decision, and succeeding generations have continued to make the same decision; therefore, as they did not desire Him, He hid His face from them. This was all He could do. No one can force himself on someone else who does not desire him. Israel did not desire Him and made her wishes very plain. Therefore, as all others, they have reaped the results. In other words, they chose to take themselves purposefully out of the hands of Jehovah and, thereby, placed themselves into the hands of Satan. The results were obvious, as such results are always obvious.

Regrettably, this scenario has not yet ended. Continuing to reject Him, Israel will, instead, accept *"another"* as their Messiah (Jn. 5:43). This will happen in the very near future and will bring Israel yet another holocaust (Mat. 24:21–22).

However, and finally, Israel will come out of the darkness into the light and will accept Christ as their Saviour and Messiah. The next passages tell us how.

MERCY

"Therefore thus says the Lord GOD; Now will I bring again the captivity of Jacob, and have mercy upon the whole house of Israel, and will be jealous for My holy name" (Ezek. 39:25).

The mercy mentioned here is made possible because of Israel's repentance—mercy will be shown to anyone who truly repents before the Lord. The Lord will always have mercy on all who will meet His conditions. To be sure, His conditions aren't stringent, but *"easy"* and *"light"* (Mat. 11:29-30).

The vision that Ezekiel had opens and closes with a valley of dry bones, for after the vultures and wild beasts shall have finished their feast, nothing but bones (the bones of the army of the Antichrist) will remain. However, for those bones, there will be no resurrection to life.

So, these two valleys contrast each other—the one, Israel, is a testimony to God's faithfulness and love; the other, the bones of the army of the Antichrist, testifies of His fidelity in judgment.

The word *now* in Ezekiel 39:25 gives us the time that this will happen. It will be after the battle of Armageddon and at the second advent of Christ. This will be the occasion of the humbling of Israel before the Lord and His lifting *"the captivity of Jacob."* That captivity has lasted now for about 2,500 years. Regrettably, none of it had to be, but it was only because of their uncleanness and transgressions. As a result, His mercy will be so extended that it will include *"the whole house of Israel"* because the whole house will repent and accept Him as their Saviour and their Lord.

The phrase, *"and will be jealous for My holy name,"* is a fearsome statement. His holy name stands behind His Word. The Lord is jealous that His honor be protected and that every single prophecy be fulfilled. And, to be sure, that it shall be.

JEALOUSY

The Lord said that He would be jealous for His holy name. The Hebrew root meaning of the word *jealousy* portrays a very strong emotion—a passionate desire. The word is used in both a positive and negative sense.

The strong emotion represented by this word can be viewed positively as a high level of commitment when it describes the feeling of a person for something that is rightly his or her own. Here, jealousy has the sense of intense love. When applied to God, jealousy communicates the fierce intensity of His commitment to His people, even when they turn from Him.

In giving the Mosaic law, the Lord announced to the people of Israel that they must remain committed to Him and not turn to idolatry, and He gave this reason for it: *"I the LORD your God am a jealous God"* (Ex. 20:5). Therefore, the jealousy of God is expressed in Old Testament history, both in punishing and in showing love.

JEALOUSY AS SHOWN IN THE OLD TESTAMENT

In the Old Testament, God is said to be jealous for His people, for His land (Joel 2:18), and for Jerusalem and Zion (Zech. 1:14). This is expressed in the New Testament, as well, respecting Israel concerning the second coming (Rev. 19).

While the anger of God is an expression of God's jealous wrath, the acts of judgment recorded in the Old Testament continue to be for the ultimate benefit of a people who must be brought back to a right relationship with God if they are to experience blessing.

Neither God nor humans are cold, computer-like beings. Persons have emotions as well as intellect and will, and often these emotions are strong. Jealousy, or zeal, is one of the stronger emotions.

God's jealousy, although it issues in punishment as well as blessing, is viewed as something both righteous and good. In general, human jealousy is viewed with suspicion. Our emotions are too often tainted by the sin that twists human personalities; however, one can experience strong emotional commitments to what is good, as well as strong emotional desires for what is not our own.

As it relates to God, jealousy is of the essence of His moral character. It is a major cause for worship and confidence on the part of His people and a ground for fear on the part of His enemies, as is given here.

DWELL SAFELY IN THEIR LAND

"After that they have borne their shame and all their trespasses whereby they have trespassed against Me, when they dwelt safely in their land, and none made them afraid" (Ezek. 39:26). This verse proclaims the reason for all of the terrible difficulties of Israel through the many centuries.

The implication of this verse is that all the shame was unnecessary. The Jews, sadly and regrettably, have carried this shame for nearly 2,000 years. They have steadfastly refused to admit that it was because of their trespasses. Consequently, many have been ashamed of their Jewishness or puzzled by the persecution, thereby, they blame Christ and Christians when, in reality, it's their own trespasses that have caused the shame.

Even though the trespasses are the cause, still, the real cause is the refusal to repent of the trespasses. Trespasses, sadly and regrettably, are incumbent upon all (Rom. 3:23). It is the lack of admittance of the trespasses and the refusal to come to Christ in order that these trespasses be handled correctly by faith in His atoning shed blood that brings judgment. Jesus said, *"And you will not come to Me, that you might have life"* (Jn. 5:40).

DAVID

In David's last song, he said, *"For I have kept the ways of the LORD, and have not wickedly departed from my God"* (II Sam. 22:22).

How could David say this at the end of his life, especially considering that he had committed a terrible sin with Bathsheba and against her husband Uriah, as well as other grievous sins?

David was not saying that he had not sinned, but that he had not wickedly departed from God's ways of handling that sin. He admitted it before the Lord and believed in the Lord, and these sins were washed away by the precious blood of Christ (II Sam. 12:13; Ps. 51).

Regarding sin, most men refuse to accept God's way, instead, devising their own ways, which the Lord will not accept.

Men attempt to atone for their sins by joining churches, becoming religious, giving money, doing good works, ad infinitum; consequently, they depart wickedly from God's ways and continue to bear the shame.

The moment one takes his sin to Christ, confesses that he is a sinner, and asks for the mercy, grace, and love of the Lord, the sin is instantly forgiven, cleansed, washed, and put away (I Jn. 1:9). This Israel would not do, and most all others will not do it either.

But finally, Israel shall. Then they will dwell safely in their land, and none shall make them afraid.

THE REGATHERING OF ISRAEL

"When I have brought them again from the people, and gathered them out of their enemies' lands, and am sanctified in them in the sight of many nations" (Ezek. 39:27). This verse proclaims the gathering that will take place after the second coming of Christ, which will include every Jew from every country in the world, who will gladly be brought to Israel.

The word *again* proclaims the fact of a second gathering, with the first having taken place beginning in 1948.

In every nation of the world, including America, the Jew is looked at, in many cases, with hostility. This is very wrong but very real.

However, the main reason this phrase, *"their enemies' lands,"* is used is because the Lord intends for all Jews to be in the land of Israel. The phrase, *"and am sanctified in them in the sight of many nations,"* refers to His plan for them finally being realized; consequently, all the promises and predictions given to the prophets will be brought to pass. Thus will the Lord be *"sanctified in them."*

RESTORATION

"Then shall they know that I am the LORD *their God, which caused them to be led into captivity among the heathen: but I have gathered them unto their own land, and have left none of them anymore there"* (Ezek. 39:28). This verse has reference to Israel finally recognizing Christ as the Messiah and Lord and Saviour. For some 2,000 years, they have steadfastly denied this fact, but *"then shall they know."* The word *then* signifies the time as the second coming of the Lord.

The phrase, *"but I have gathered them unto their own land,"* proclaims the fact that so certain is the future restoration of Israel that the past tense is used here in predicting it.

The phrase, *"and have left none of them anymore there,"* refers to lands other than Israel.

As well, this will not be a forced return but a joyful return, inasmuch as most, if not all, will accept Christ at this time.

Understanding that their Messiah has really come, the news is going to spread around the world in record time. Consequently, every Jew on the face of the earth at that time will begin to make plans to move to Israel. This will be at the beginning of the kingdom age when our Lord will rule the entirety of the world as King of kings and Lord of lords. In other words, every official on the face of the earth will answer to Him; consequently, there will be no more war, no more hunger, no more pain or sickness, no more racism, and no more little children crying in the ghettos. It will be a time of peace and prosperity, and a time of blessing such as the world has never known in all of its history, which God originally intended for it to be. Please believe me, it is definitely going to happen.

THE POURED OUT SPIRIT

"Neither will I hide My face anymore from them: for I have poured out My Spirit upon the house of Israel, says the Lord GOD*"* (Ezek. 39:29). This verse proclaims that which will be done because Israel has now accepted Christ as Lord and Saviour.

The Spirit of God cannot be poured out on anyone until first the sin question is settled, which can only be done by the individual evidencing faith in Christ and what Christ has done at the cross.

The balance of the chapters in Ezekiel have to do with the coming kingdom age, the rebuilding of the millennial temple, etc. All of this proves that Ezekiel 38 and 39 are, in fact, a portrayal of the battle of Armageddon. The chronology demands this.

Ezekiel 37 proclaims Israel being brought back as a nation, with Ezekiel 38 and 39 portraying the advent of the Antichrist in his efforts to destroy Israel, which will culminate in the battle of Armageddon. That will precipitate the second coming of the Lord, with Jesus then reigning in Jerusalem in the restored nation and rebuilt temple.

How do I know my sin's forgiven?
My Saviour tells me so;
That now I am an heir of heaven?
My Saviour tells me so.

By trusting Christ the witness came,
My Saviour tells me so;
The pardon's free in Jesus' name,
My Saviour tells me so.

Believe and you shall surely live,
My Saviour tells me so;
The Spirit's witness God will give,
My Saviour tells me so.

Though rough the way, I shall endure,
My Saviour tells me so;
His sheep are ever kept secure,
My Saviour tells me so.

How do I know I'll live again?
My Saviour tells me so;
With Christ in glory I shall reign,
My Saviour tells me so.

Away with doubt, away with fear;
When this by faith I know;
God's Word shall stand forevermore,
My Saviour tells me so.

REFERENCES

INTRO

George Williams, *William's Complete Bible Commentary*, Grand Rapids, Kregel Publications, 1994.

CHAPTER 1

[1] George Williams, *William's Complete Bible Commentary*, Grand Rapids, Kregel Publications, 1994, Pg. 605.

CHAPTER 3

[1] George Williams, *William's Complete Bible Commentary*, Grand Rapids, Kregel Publications, 1994, Pg. 606.

[2] George Williams, *William's Complete Bible Commentary*, Grand Rapids, Kregel Publications, 1994, Pg. 607.

ABOUT EVANGELIST JIMMY SWAGGART

The Rev. Jimmy Swaggart is a Pentecostal evangelist whose anointed preaching and teaching has drawn multitudes to the cross of Christ since 1955.

As an author, he has written more than 60 books, commentaries, study guides, and The Expositor's Study Bible, which has sold more than 4 million copies.

As an award-winning musician and singer, Brother Swaggart has recorded more than 60 gospel albums and sold nearly 17 million recordings worldwide.

For more than six decades, Brother Swaggart has channeled his preaching and music ministry through multiple media venues including print, radio, television and the Internet.

In 2010, Jimmy Swaggart Ministries launched its own cable channel, SonLife Broadcasting Network, which airs 24 hours a day to a potential viewing audience of more than 2 billion people around the globe.

Brother Swaggart also pastors Family Worship Center in Baton Rouge, Louisiana, the church home and headquarters of Jimmy Swaggart Ministries.

Jimmy Swaggart Ministries materials can be found at **www.jsm.org**.

ALSO BY EVANGELIST
JIMMY SWAGGART

(09-158) AMAZING GRACE – AN AUTOBIOGRAPHY BY JIMMMY SWAGGART
(09-138) THE FUTURE OF ISRAEL
(09-163) HOW THE HOLY SPIRIT WORKS
(09-139) DIVINE HEALING
(09-156) THE RESURRECTION

AVAILABLE AT SHOPJSM.ORG